SINCE TIME BEGAN

The Truths and the Myths
About Sexual Orientation

Virginia Schroeder Burnham
In Collaboration With
William H. Hampton, M.D.

SUNSTONE
PRESS

SANTA FE
NEW MEXICO

First edition

Printed in the United States of America

Library of Congress Cataloging in Publication Data

Burnham, Virginia Schroeder , 1908-
      Since time began : the truths and the myths about sexual
   orientation / Virginia Schroeder Burnham. – 1st ed.
         p.   cm.
      ISBN 0-86534-199-0 $9.95
      1. Homosexuality.   2. Sexual orientaton.   3. Gender identity.
   I. Title.
   HQ76.25.B87   1994
   306.76–dc20   94-38981
                                                                        CIP

Published by Sunstone Press
            Post Office Box 2321
            Santa Fe, New Mexico 87504-2321 / USA
            (505) 988-4418 / *FAX: (505) 988-1025*
            orders only (800) 243-5644

TABLE OF CONTENTS

Introduction

Homosexuality is often referred to as an alternate form of sexuality. That definition makes sense to non-homosexuals who see homosexuality as an "alternate" to their own form of sexuality. However, for gay and lesbian people, homosexuality is not an alternative. It is the only form of sexuality which we have. Many of the problems our culture has developed in its view of homosexuality are rooted in the fact that until recently, everyone was consulted about homosexuality except homosexuals themselves. The result has been a quagmire of ignorance and misinformation.

In the pages which follow, my good friend, the author, sets about the task of lifting our understanding of homosexuality from the dark pit of taboo and superstition into the light of reason, fact, compassion and wisdom, not to mention truth. Her book draws not only on the actual experiences of homosexuals themselves, but also upon the most recent research on homosexuality. She thus helps her reader to gain an understanding that is based on fact, not on preconceived prejudices. As a people, Americans have rarely dealt with their sexuality in the same straight-forward manner in which they deal with their other biological and emotional urges such as hunger or the need for friendship. Whether it be homosexuality or heterosexuality, Americans have all too often responded to human sexuality with fear, avoidance, deception, condemnation and punishment.

Our culture has tended to believe that sexuality is an "enemy within" which must be controlled and suppressed until we enter into heterosexual marriage. Our society has traditionally taught that the same sexuality which leads the unmarried person to sin and evil is suddenly transformed by marriage into a doorway to joy and holiness. Of course, that transformation is only possible for heterosexual forms of sexuality. In other words, instead of seeing our sexuality as a gift to be used responsibly, Americans tend to see sex as being governed by random taboos and not by mature, responsible stewardship. Thankfully, this peculiar view is now being re-examined.

Until recently, most Americans went through life completely unaware that the majority of them were in the company of gay men and lesbians every day. Prior to the 1960s, the social, legal, and religious punishments which were leveled against those who were exposed as homosexuals were so horrific that most homosexuals concealed their sexual identity. With few real life examples to challenge the conventional wisdom of society, most Americans have simply accepted as fact the cultural myths and folklore about homosexual persons. Sadly, most of this folklore is highly inaccurate, falsely presenting homosexuals as mentally deranged, dangerous monsters.

The latter half of the 20th century in America has seen an incredible leap in the communication of knowledge to every level of society. Whether it be through computer bulletin boards or cable TV, our minds now have almost instantaneous access to facts and information that were formerly available only to academics and research specialists, if at all. When I was coming to grips with my homosexuality as a child in the Texas of the 1950s, it was almost impossible to find any information on homosexuality other than a few technical references in dictionaries and medical books. Mention of the subject was virtually banned from the mass media. I was ten years old before I even heard another human being say the word "homosexual." I was in college before I began to comprehend that there were actually other people like myself. More importantly, I began to discover that many of the long sought "others like me" were people I had known for years without realizing that they were also homosexual.

That situation has dramatically changed in the last few decades. Today, homosexual characters in movies, plays, TV, etc., give realistic portrayals of gay and lesbian life. Even the president of the United States and other prominent Americans speak openly of a desire to help homosexuals win acceptance and freedom from fear, violence and persecution. Homosexuals who once lived in terror of exposure are now networking with each other and discovering that they are not alone. Many heterosexual persons are now discovering that the once "hated and feared homosexual" is their own child, best friend or beloved coworker. Myth, fear, superstition and ignorance are no longer acceptable when you finally realize that the person in question is someone whom you love and respect deeply. As peoples' fears and prejudices are now being confronted by the real life experiences of people they know and love, they have begun to search for real and concrete answers.

In this book, the author provides many of those answers. Her work is a welcome attempt to gather the current facts about homosexuality into a form that can be easily understood and assimilated. Of course, some of the data is still in dispute. No one book will ever be able to give a presentation of this complex subject which would be fully acceptable to every reader. But unquestionably, the author has set us on the right road and pointed us in the right direction. She asks nothing more of her readers than a dedication to fairness and a desire to know the truth.

As a Christian priest, I believe that sexuality is a gift from God. Our sexuality is not some "enemy within" which we must battle or flee from less it destroy us. Our sexuality is an inseparable part of human nature. It is a tool that we must use as good stewards just as we must be good stewards of all the gifts with which the Creator has blessed us. Just as we use and express our material wealth, our strength of body, our intelligence of mind and our various creative abilities, so must we also exercise mature stewardship over our sexuality. The thoughtful and insightful information in this book will be a great help to every reader who truly wants to understand their homosexual friends and relatives or their own sexuality. I am thankful to Virginia for offering the healing gift of this book to us all.

As you read, may the Eternal grant you discernment, stillness and peace,

Father James Lee Walker
Christ Church Episcopal
Greenwich, Connecticut
September, 1994

Preface

My purpose in writing this book is to help set the record straight regarding the different kinds of sexuality some men and women have. At no other time in history has there been more public discussion about homosexuality. The press and television abound in programs on the subject and differing opinions are bandied about, some right and some wrong. In this book we tell you all we know to be true and admit what we don't know.

As you read you ask yourself, why do I bother? Don't I know all I need to know about homosexuality? Or perhaps you are just curious or perhaps you are gay and want to know what we say about it. You may have already formed an opinion but would like to see if there is anything new.

If you are heterosexual, as most people are, maybe you reject the gay community and their activist demands. But, whatever you are, straight, bisexual or gay, please read on and allow the information to enlighten you about sexual orientation.

There have been homosexual men and women since recorded history. A count has never been taken but it is estimated that about ten percent of the male population and four percent of women are gay. This number is disputed up and down, but until an official count is made we can only guess, which can only be done when they are accepted totally into our society.

Then you ask, why are there gays? The answer is, we don't know. We do know, however, that to be homosexual is not a matter of choice by the individual. Homosexuals are born gay and exhibit gay behavior in varying degrees throughout a lifetime. Your next door neighbor may be, or the waitperson in the restaurant. You may never know because it is difficult to detect as only a small percentage are obviously gay and society has put a stigma on them and most remain unrecognized by choice. Some gays, both men and women, marry and have children and are good parents and spouses. They are good citizens and have the same birthrights as the rest of us, and many make important contributions to the world.

The homosexual population is a minority group as are several others in our world. This poses a challenge to them and to us and is a question of understanding and acceptance on the part of both. So, in our opinion, it is only fair to allow gays to live their lives as straights do, without belittling, criticizing, and judging them.

I could not have written this book without the counsel of the Rev. James Lee Walker, who guided me from the beginning to the end with his advice. I wish to acknowledge the gays, with my appreciation and thanks, who divulged their innermost emotions regardng their sexual orientation. And last but not least, my heartfelt thanks go to Rob Pincus for the advice he gave me on the title of this book from the standpoint of a straight and for his help in the promotion of my books.

CHAPTER ONE
What Is Homosexuality?

The sexuality most of us know is heterosexuality. In other words, sex between a man and a woman. Homosexuality is a variation directed toward a person of the same sex, a man desires another man and a woman another woman. The homosexual man or woman is not attracted to a person of the opposite sex as are heterosexuals.

The prefixes of the word sexuality, "hetero" and "homo," are derived from the Greek, hetero meaning "different" and homo meaning the "same." Most think that "homo" refers to "man" but this is not so; it means the "same" and is used in the English as a prefix in several words, such as homogeneous, homogenize and homonym. A man is referred to as being "gay" and a woman as "lesbian," although gay is also used for a woman.

HOW MANY ARE THERE?

As mentioned in the preface, it is estimated that ten percent of males and four percent of females are gay, and this estimate may be low. These figures originated from the research by Kinsey in the 1940s. He included in his study all kinds of sexual activity that occurred in a man's life from when he was a young boy fraternizing with other boys, studying erotic pictures, giggling over eroticisms and masturbating together. These activities were included in the ten percent and should not have been.

Many homosexuals claim that there are far more than ten percent and indeed, there are clusters, particularly of gay men, in areas of the country and in certain fields of endeavor, notably the performing and creative arts, designing, painting, dancing and so forth. However, such talents are not the domain exclusively of the gay community as a sphere of work.

In regard to female homosexuality, Kinsey reports from his studies that the range varies fairly widely from one to ten percent depending on the age of the individual and her marital status, single, married, separated, widowed or divorced. There were a few cases of homosexual females who were married and never had sexual relations with their husbands, but they maintained the marriage for social and/or monetary reasons. Sexual conduct of both lay outside the marriage.

Financial and other circumstances often bring single women to live together and Kinsey's broad research clearly indicates that while the larger majority of such households never involve homosexual activity, those that do are heterosexual individuals.

As with the male gay, it is impossible to state the specific percentage of lesbians in the population as so many variables enter into any calculation.

SOME APPEAR TO BE BUT ARE NOT

There are many variations of homosexuality, even to the point that a man may be homosexual in activity but not in orientation or history. Some of these men are weak, passive individuals, unable to make a living, or any kind of vocational progress, or to establish themselves comfortably financially and emotionally. They have families but are not interested in being involved with them and somehow become caught up in some degree of homosexual activity as a social outlet and personal way of life.

At times, they live with a homosexual, sometimes alone and engage in sexual activity with their homosexual friends. In this fashion these passive men cope with their sexual drive in an almost mentally retarded way. They will submit to almost anything their lovers request in order to keep their friendship, and to maintain their niche in life. They consider this manner of living a lifesaver in order to exist.

There is also a group of men who claim that they are gay. They are afflicted with schizophrenia, a mental disorder controlled by medication. However, they very rarely engage in sexual play of any kind, and if they take their medication and go for psychotherapy they can operate in a normal manner.

Then there is the man in jail who has no release for his sexual drive. He submits to anal sex because there is no other outlet available, but he is not homosexual. When he is out of jail and finds a place in the straight community, he will behave perfectly normally. I may be making too many generalities, but there are many variations of homosexual activity by men who are not homosexual.

HOMOSEXUALITY IS INBORN

Since when have we known about homosexuality? Gays have been with us since the evolvement of the human race and are referred to in every language since recorded history. Some people consider them abnormal and others regard homosexuality as an illness. Some condemn gays as immoral, that they are doing wrong and should be despised. Homosexuality should not be thought of as any of these things. It is simply a phenomenon of nature.

There are people who malign the homosexual, man or woman, and blame them for choosing his or her sexual preference. This is wrong. Homosexuality is not a matter of choice but a fundamental fact of personality that is inborn. Ask any gay person at what age he or she was aware of being different. Some will say they knew when they were three or four, others at puberty, during adolescence or even approaching middle age. So the general public focuses only on the sexual element of personality in the judgment of an individual who is gay.

Although homosexuality was condoned and accepted in ancient cultures, in our civilization it is considered for the most part an illegal, covert, contemptible activity. But the fact is clear. No homosexual asked to be or wanted to be gay. Rather, the shoe is on the other foot, for some have desired to change and have gone to great lengths and others, coerced by family, friends and the pressures of society to be "reverted" to heterosexuality have also gone this route. This will be discussed in depth in Chapter 4.

THERE ARE MANY DEGREES

It is the opinion of most people that a person is either completely heterosexual or homosexual. This is not the case. It is true that some men and women are wholly heterosexual and some homosexual but the fact remains that in a considerable proportion of the population, as we have already explained, it is a matter of degree in each individual how much is gay and how much is straight in both actual experience and/or psychic response. There are some men and women whose heterosexual experiences predominate and some whose homosexual experiences do, and some who have equal amounts. The timing of these alternating types of sexual behavior varies widely in each individual. There is no set pattern, one day it could be gay, the next or even the same day, straight or vice versa. The Kinsey studies show that two men out of five of the total male population have had overt homosexual experience between adolescence and old age.

So now let us accept the fact that gays do not choose their sexual orientation. Nevertheless, does a gay man ever find negative aspects to the condition he was born into? Yes, there are several and all are imposed by society. First is the persecution, then the lack of children, which for some gays is fulfilled. Then there is the impossibility of marriage with a beloved partner with the civil rights afforded straights, and lastly, the necessity for most to live in the "silent ghetto."

WHY ARE THEY CALLED "GAY"?

How did the word "gay" develop to describe the homosexual? It is sometimes spelled "gai," and is widely used today in French, Dutch, Danish, Japanese, Swedish and other languages with the same meaning as in English. However, there is general reluctance on the part of academics to use the word, probably due to their disinclination to employ popular language.

The use of "gay" antedates centuries in recorded history and is spotted in the thirteenth and fourteenth. The word "homosexual" was coined in the late nineteenth century by German psychologists and introduced into the English language in the beginning of the twentieth, where it was vehemently opposed because of its vague connotations. Notwithstanding, "gay" was used in the subculture as a sort of password or code with which to communicate with one another and identify a common bond, as society had made it difficult for so long for gays to be open about their sexual orientation, to be understood and accepted for what they are. So the word "gay" remained sub rosa in the United States until 1939 when Cary Grant appeared in the movie "Bringing up Baby" wearing a dress, and exclaimed that he had "gone gay."

And what about the word "straight" for the heterosexual? This word is commonly used in the vernacular as the antithesis of gay, but has no historical background and its connotations are less specific, but it is utilized as a companion to gay at this point in history. In general usage, it is indefinite in its meaning and may connote a stodgy, dull person who walks the straight and narrow path in life and never kicks over the traces.

THERE ARE DIFFERENT KINDS

Different types of homosexuality apply to both men and women. One is exclusively homosexual, another is bisexual and a small group recently identified by Masters and Johnson is "ambisexual." The male bisexual often falls in love with a woman, marries and has children, the lesbian with a man and also raises a family, the ambisexual may be a male or a female and enjoys sexual relations with anyone who responds to him or her. Such a person is equally comfortable with a partner of either sex. Each of these categories will be described later. So it is clear that there is a wide variety of the degree of sexual preference in both men and women and all were born that way.

However, the bisexual gay man has a problem with sex in that he thinks a good deal about it and has a great amount of sexual vigor, but finds it physiologically difficult to function with the opposite sex. He is not bisexual in the sense that he is equally capable with either sex, it is that he can function with the opposite sex, but prefers the same sex in a homosexual fashion. For him, it is much more pleasant, relaxing and successful, but he is able to perform to some degree with the opposite sex. Such men often marry and have children.

YOUR CAN'T TELL A GAY BY THE LOOKS

Some straight people claim that they can detect a male homosexual by his mannerisms and looks, in other words, body language. In fact, physical traits that are considered homosexual are noticeable in only fifteen percent of males and five percent of females. So, homosexuals cannot be identified with any certainty. Superficial features, such as mannerisms, posturing and clothing are not necessarily indicative, nor is the voice, body movement or appearance. Gays are offended by being pointed out on this basis and heterosexuals are also troubled by faulty identification.

Lesbians seem to be more healthy psychologically than gay males and more able to cope with society, probably because they are not suspect as some men are who go into lines of work in which gay men predominate. However, that may be changing, as more and more women apply and are hired for jobs that it was believed only men could perform. Examples are fire fighters, pilots in the military, truck drivers, professionals and so forth.

During the past few decades, homosexuals have become more overt in behavior as social mores began to relax. Much of the way they act is natural, but there are those who put it on to challenge society or to attract partners. A few may flaunt a supercilious, antagonistic style which is characteristic of their worst features, the aggressiveness of the male and the bitchiness of the female. These men are often the ectomorphic type, tall and slight of build, less often of the mesomorphic, muscular build. They are usually artistic, preferring occupations that call for creativity. A lesbian may be masculine in appearance and have male mannerisms and wear manly clothes, but these are very few.

HOW DO GAYS FEEL ABOUT THEMSELVES?

Depending on personality, the more "thinking" person feels guilt, shame, self-hate and humiliation, all resulting in anger. This may continue as an underlying structure for life or may become alleviated with acceptance and companionship, bringing love and happiness through maturity. The more "doing" gay may debase him or herself for being different, but never feels it is a problem, works it out and goes on with life. However, they all go through the rejection by society and learn how to handle it, each in his and her way. How it is handled depends largely on whether or not he or she is in or "out of the closet." Being out of the closet is a much more comfortable way of life for gays, for once they are out they feel they can be themselves and can adjust to the environment or move into one where homosexuality is considered normal.

Although straights are for the most part unaware of their presence, the gay man and woman is constantly mindful that they are different and seldom feel comfortable in a group of straights. As one gay man put it: "From earliest childhood, I lived in a 'silent ghetto' and couldn't understand why."

DO GAYS HAVE DIFFERENT PERSONALITIES THAN STRAIGHTS?

Aside from sexual orientation, there are subtle differences between the straight man and the gay man. The gay has much more of the nurturing and caring component in his makeup. It is not that the straight has none, but it is of a different quality. For instance, a gay man finds it easier and more comfortable than a straight to be a nurse and to serve people in a personal way, such as hairdressing, physical therapy, massage and such occupations that associate them with another person's body. This type of work is pleasing, satisfying and more rewarding. Hands on involvement seems to be natural to gays whereas many straights would be uncomfortable in that area.

Gay men also veer toward the aesthetic in which to make a living and to enjoy it. It is not that they preempt this domain for there are many fine straights who are aesthetic and very masculine. However, for some reason gays look on music, dance, theater and the arts in general as their bailiwick and in some ways try to dominate these disciplines.

Many straights feel that gays indulge in sex a great deal more than they do, probably because some gays are apt to boast openly about their sexual contacts. It is evident from scientific studies that there are degrees of sexual desire in any individual, straight or gay, male or female, from very high to very low in the general population, regardless of gender or sexual orientation. Some women, such as prostitutes, are known to have sexual relations thirty or forty times a day, and there are men who have eight to twelve orgasms in a day. These are extremes and not indicative of homosexual, bisexual or heterosexual activity.

WHAT ARE DOCTORS TAUGHT ABOUT HOMOSEXUALITY?

There is little in the core curriculum, as the subject of homosexuality falls into the category of mental conditions. Psychiatric students were taught that homosexuality is a mental disorder, although it has been recognized since recorded history and accepted in many cultures over the centuries.

Medical students were given information that is biased, inaccurate and inappropriate. A regimen called "separative therapy" was taught, whereby the homosexual could be changed to a heterosexual. As we now know through experience, this is not feasible and the therapy can cause irreparable damage to the psyche of the individual.

So in 1973, the American Psychiatric Association removed from its manual homosexuality as a mental disorder. Notwithstanding, homophobia persists, especially in men, and individual bias is difficult to dislodge. It seems to be very difficult for men to accept this form of sexuality. In fact, most don't, nor do they make an attempt to do so. Women are far more open minded, accepting and understanding of the gay man and lesbian.

Today, there is still a conflict between psychiatrists as to how they view homosexuality and their training remains far from adequate in this regard. In fact, training in human sexuality per se is scarce, for there is little scientific data upon which to base it.

CHAPTER TWO
How Does Society React To Gays?

HISTORY FROM ANCIENT DAYS
Throughout history, homosexuals have been subjected to judgment ranging from total acceptance to total rejection. In ancient Greece and Roman days, homosexuals were accepted and they commingled freely with the rest of the population. There was a high rate in both countries of homosexual activity and men bought and sold young boys to satisfy their sexual needs. Hero and Caligula, both Ceasars, were homosexual, and male prostitutes were numerous and accepted by society. Since then, about the time of the advent of Christianity, homosexuals have not enjoyed this liberality, for around 300 A.D., laws were enacted banning the practice of homosexuality, and anal intercourse was punishable by death.

The early history of homosexuality in this country is also liberal, for it is known that the American Plains Indians considered male homosexuals valuable members of the household and the community. Families adopted them to do the work of a woman with a man's strength and there is no record of lack of acceptance or rejection by the braves. From then on matters became more difficult for homosexuals, especially as Christianity became widespread.

By the eleventh century, the Catholic church punished homosexual priests and monks severely and in some instances by death, and by 1600 in England, their goods and land were taken. By the beginning of the nineteenth century, Napoleon relaxed the laws in France and homosexual acts between consenting adults were condoned, but England and the United States remained adamant and reinforced them. By this time, the laws in most countries were directed against the male homosexual and lesbianism was regarded as non-existent.

WHAT ARE THE LAWS TODAY?

Today, the United States continues to have repressive laws about homosexuality, while many western countries have relaxed them, including England, France, Holland, Italy, Spain, the Scandinavian countries and several in South America. In the United States, being homosexual is not illegal, but performing sexual acts and soliciting sexual favors is. Also, the states differ in respect to the laws, but most adhere to sodomy and soliciting favors as misdemeanors or felonies. In addition, men and women homosexuals are denied civil rights in housing and employment. They are discriminated against in credit, insurance, and child custody, and neither have the privilege of marrying and receiving the tax and legal benefits or property and inheritance rights associated with legally sanctioned unions.

Thus, in the course of human history most cultures have been and still are more accepting of heterosexuality than of homosexuality. However, some are not particularly opposed, and some even condone homosexual behavior in young males before marriage and even after marriage, but heterosexuality is the most accepted form of sexuality.

HOW DO THE JUDEO-CHRISTIAN RELIGIONS REACT?

How did this discrimination against homosexuals happen? Judeo-Christian teachings are from the Bible and religious leaders and scholars have interpreted them. Actually, the scriptures relate the practices of homosexuality per se as evil and contrary to the will of God and not individuals with homosexual orientation. Only males are mentioned and females only in passing. The interpretation of the scriptures by the hierarchy connotes otherwise and has resulted in the condemnation by many people of gay men and women.

What does the Christian religion tell us about homosexuality? There are several interpretations pro and con and in varying degrees of total rejection to total acceptance in which there is little if any common ground. This causes a great deal of confusion and some hostility relating to the interpretation by various sectors of society, hence controversy prevails. So let us examine what the

Bible is rather than what it says. The Bible is a collection of human experiences shared with God. It is not a set of rules for humankind set down by God.

In the writings of the ancient Hebrews and in all the ancient languages in which the Bible was written, there were many allusions to "homosexual behavior" but never written were the words "homosexuality" or "homosexual orientation."

The scriptural texts in the Bible most relevant to homosexuality are in Paul's letters. First, we find that it is not an important matter. The earliest Hebrews make no mention of it nor do the Ten Commandments, the four gospels of Jesus say nothing about it, and there were no words in Hebrew or ancient Greek to describe homosexuality. So obviously it was not of concern.

In fact, the term homosexuality was not coined until after 1850 by a Hungarian writer and came into usage in English only toward the end of the nineteenth century. Heretofore, there was no mention of homosexuality in the King James version of 1612 and the first use of the term in an English Bible finally came in 1946 in the revised standard version of the New Testament. In subsequent editions the word was dropped or changed in 1971 and 1973 in favor of "homosexual perversion."

Therefore, there are no clear and specific answers to the question of homosexual behavior in the voluminous theological writings of the period when the written word came into being, both before and since the coming of Christ.

WHAT IS SODOMY?

Where do the words sodomy and sodomite come from? From the ancient city of Sodom. The act of anal intercourse was named sodomy and the man enacting it, a sodomite. According to Genesis 19, these words were coined from an anecdote that took place in Lot's house in Sodom. Two angels, disguised as men, were offered hospitality in Lot's house as was the custom in those times. After dinner, a crowd of men came to Lot's house and asked that the guests be brought to them because they wanted to "know" them. The word "know" in Hebrew referred to sexual relations and is so used in the Bible today. Lot offered his virgin daughters, but they were declined.

The men of Sodom then proceeded to violate Lot and his guests. The assault ceased only when the guests caused the men to be blinded, and they advised Lot to leave Sodom because the Lord was about to destroy the city, which He did that night. The next morning Sodom and nearby Gomorrah were nothing but smoking ruins.

WESTERN SOCIETY IS RELAXING THE RULES SOMEWHAT

During the past fifteen years, religious groups have begun to slacken their hold on the rights and wrongs of homosexuality. The conservative and reformed groups of Judaism are accepting homosexuals with compassion and understanding, although still adhering to the fundamental writings of the Talmud. Several Protestant groups are relenting in their opinion of homosexuals and a few accept their civil rights, even to including them as worthy of receiving the privileges offered by the church and the community at large.

It is admitted by members of most religious denominations that there are many homosexual men active and working within the church and serving the community with no questions asked. Nevertheless, the Roman Catholic church remains unyielding in its disapproval and censure of homosexuality in any form. Moreover, we have a very powerful religious right, a huge conservative block, particularly in the Roman Catholic and southern Baptist traditions where these groups see homosexuality as a sin, a biblical, prohibitive sin. Therefore, they tend to militate against homosexuals, which has been backed up by laws in the past. As recently as two generations ago, a homosexual was apprehended, arrested, jailed and all his possessions sold for having sex with another man. There are areas in this country where such laws still exist although most have been done away with.

SOME GROUPS REMAIN ADAMANT

Only recently the state of Colorado enacted a law that homosexuals cannot legally be recognized as a group entitled to protection in the same way as racial minorities, thus voiding any law that guarantees such rights. This news aroused a storm of protest from individuals and groups around the country. Several Hollywood celebrities endorsed a boycott on vacations there and denounced Colorado's "vote for hate." Many organizations canceled scheduled conventions and several large cities barred municipal travel to the state.

One of the most strident opponents of the homosexual community is the relatively recent religious right. Back in the early 1980s when the dreadful plague of acquired immune deficiency syndrome (AIDS) emerged and the Western world became aware of it, it appeared that this dreadful disease was visited primarily on homosexuals. Pressed by the religious right, newscasters broadcast the fact that the disease started in homosexuals. Very soon, this notion was dispelled, and now we know the truth, that AIDS is a fatal disease and has no correlation with the gay community. At that time, however, it was bandied about by the religious right that AIDS was a scourge visited by God upon homosexuals specifically in order to eliminate them. Some people believe that all religions in the world condemn homosexuality.

OUR CULTURE IS AMBIVALENT

Homosexuality is distorted and misunderstood in our culture. Straight men are apt to despise gays because they cannot tolerate even the thought of another man touching them in a sexual manner or pressing his penis into the mouth or rectum. This disgusts them, may frighten them and make them angry, because they resent the implication that others might think they would do such a thing. This makes the very subject of homosexuality replete with natural antagonism and rage. This starts at a very young age because young boys play with one another in sexual ways but there is a natural, innate revulsion and they pull back from it right away.

Young boys may experiment in a rather crude manner in their play and gays view this as a homosexual bent, but this is not true.

WHAT IS HOMOPHOBIA?

Homophobia is a dislike of gays, bordering on revulsion. It is unwarranted but does exist and can take many forms, such as the fear of some people that being with a gay person will make them gay and that others will think they are gay too, or will trigger the desire to be gay. Some believe that all gays are promiscuous and should not be allowed the privileges that straights enjoy, such as civil and social rights and no discrimination.

GAYS ARE BECOMING MORE VISIBLE

During the past few years there has occurred a sudden prominence of gays and much of this is due to the gays themselves, who are more open about their homosexuality and more aggressive about requesting a place in society as a minority group. However, coming out of the closet is still a risk of real harm, and the espousal of gays by President Clinton for acceptance in the military only propelled the subject further into public view. This resulted in program after program on radio and television, in periodicals and news papers, thus exposing the widely diverse pros and cons of public opinion.

All of this bodes well for gays, but there is a downside. The opposition is well-organized and forging ahead with an out and out campaign to influence the legislators of many states and the federal government to enact laws that discriminate against gays and lesbians.

GAYS IN THE MILITARY?

Getting back to President Clinton's espousal of gays in the military, he finally won his point when in 1993 the Congress approved his "don't ask, don't tell" policy and a law was passed to that effect. Heretofore, at the recruiting office, men and women were asked if they were gay, and if the answer was "yes" he or she was not allowed to join. Some lied when asked but once they were in and somehow were found out, they were dismissed summarily with a dishonorable discharge which branded them for life. Worst of all were the witch hunts for homosexuals which involved delving into the most intimate facets of a person's life at the slightest sign. Seldom was there a discharge for misconduct and most were discharged simply for being found to be gay. However, regardless of the law that was passed, there is still a great deal of dissension and eventually, the matter will go to the Supreme Court.

SO THE BASHING CONTINUES

On my desk are four appeals for money that arrived in the last mail. Two of them ask me to petition my congressional representatives not to vote for the bill granting the same legal rights to homosexuals that we heterosexuals enjoy. Another questions: "Do you want to give special rights to sodomites?"

HOW DO STRAIGHTS FEEL?

In regard to the straight community, women are more apt to accept gays whom they know or encounter or meet socially. As one woman put it: "I like to go out with gay men. They are intelligent, charming and good company and when they take you home they don't try to pull your clothes off!" From a straight man's standpoint, however, how he feels about gays may differ according to his age, his geographic location and what he has learned from his family and the society around him. But he may feel uncomfortable with a man he knows is homosexual until he gets to know him.

There are ethnic groups that are very hostile to gays and others that are fairly tolerant. Thus the controversy rages on between total acceptance and total rejection, resulting in a situation posing a challenge, both in our acceptance of them and they of us. It is not the question of discrimination but of understanding and acceptance.

Although there has always existed antagonism, especially by straight males, it seems that never has it been so blatant as in these days of openness about sexuality and intimate feelings on personal subjects. The continuous rejection and bashing of homosexuals by the Roman Catholic church, the brouhaha about gays in the military and the controversy as to whether or not the subject of homosexuality be taught in the schools has contributed to a division of society with no room for compromise.

DOCTOR OFFERS HIS VIEW

"I first became aware that there was such a person as a homosexual when I was about sixteen. As I played with friends, I found out later that one was homosexual. We all made fun of him because he was prissy and didn't want to play with us but preferred to read or do something by himself. He didn't seem to want to be one of the gang but did his own thing in his own way. Furthermore, he tended to be critical of us and the rough housing which we enjoyed as most boys do. As he matured, he developed his own life-style and we saw little of him. Later I learned that he wound up in France, was a successful editor of a newspaper and seldom came to this country. Apparently, he fell into a group of his own kind and enjoyed a satisfying life."

The doctor continues: "My experience with homosexuals stems from my teachers, the Boy Scouts and other male groups to which I belong, contacts in the army and approaches on the street. These were not aggressive, nor was I ever offended to the point of feeling I would like to attack him. For the most part, it amounted to a man laying a hand on my arm or back waiting for the response that would determine whether I would be agreeable to an encounter. However, whenever such an event occurred, mild though it may have been, I always experienced a feeling of uneasiness and of being threatened.

"Notwithstanding my experience, however, most men feel very on edge when dealing with a homosexual. Perhaps I am immune because I have a good deal of experience with them as a physician and in pursuing my hobbies of art and antiques, which fields gays often pursue. But when I am with one, I always sense my guard rising, preparing me to let him know in no uncertain terms that I will not tolerate what he is proposing in the event he makes the slightest move in that direction."

GAYS PRESENT A DILEMMA TO STRAIGHT MEN

Straight men are inundated with mixed emotions in regard to homosexuality and they are very difficult to handle in a manner that is fair. Some feel sorry for gays, yet detest them. Some want to be kind and forgiving because they are born this way, yet they don't want to have sexual favors pressed upon them. Some gays have no discretion in this regard and some are very private, yet those who are aggressive go out of their way to present themselves and may be assaultive. This depends on the personality of the individual involved and whether he is more of a thinker or a doer.

A case in point is that of the famous ice skater who was knocked out in Central Park. He was with a bunch of gays and approached two other guys thinking they were part of his group which met there every day looking for companions for sexual activity. This time, however, he made a mistake as they were straight and they hit him over the head and knocked him out. This pertains as well to the leather jacket motorcycle-riding gays who flaunt their homosexuality and ride in the parade every year in New York, and there is the act-up group who may attack someone who has expressed a dislike for gays.

So there are gays who are the passive types and others the challenging, aggressive types. These excessive "doing" types of personality are the most difficult to deal with.

THERE ARE MANY MYTHS

Misconceptions about homosexuals are rampant. Here are some myths that have been around for years. Some people think that gay men really want to be women and that lesbians want to be men, and that they can change to heterosexuality if they really want to. Some believe gays are more creative than straights and that being gay is a matter of choice. Many people think that homosexuality is contagious and by associating with gay people you can be persuaded to become gay. None of this is true.

Furthermore many people are afraid that it is dangerous for young children to be around gays, such as a teacher or a Boy Scout leader, and that children should not be allowed to associate with them. A firm belief held by some is that young children exposed to gay people will cause them to develop as homosexuals. They also believe that most child molesters are gay. Again, all this is not true. Over ninety percent of the molesters are heterosexual. In some localities this ancient myth prevents gay men and women from holding jobs such as teaching and supervising youth groups.

WHAT ARE THE LEGAL IMPLICATIONS?

Social mores in this country have succeeded in passing many

laws and regulations in regard to homosexual activity, particularly sexual perversion, including the decision of the Supreme Court that enables a state to impose restrictions on the homosexual community within its borders, as Colorado recently did.

The legal aspects of homosexuality in this country are strict in every state. While a law cannot prohibit homosexuality per se, laws can and do prohibit and enforce laws against certain activities of homosexual relations. However, in every culture there are only isolated cases of legal action taken against lesbians for homosexual activity in recorded history.

Kinsey postulates that his many studies determine that a large percentage of the male population has had at least one sexual experience to orgasm with another male when he was young. This amounts to about one third of the male population.

AND HOW DO GAYS FEEL?

There is a quasi militant group of male homosexuals and lesbians who are constantly in the public eye in one location or another. They demonstrate loudly and demand the same civil and legal rights that the straight community enjoys. They ask for acceptance as members of the human race but do not ask for approval of what they do in the privacy of their homes.

Gays also are sensitive to the labels that are put upon them, such as "sexual preference." This implies that they chose homosexuality, which is not the case. Homosexuality is an inborn fact of life that cannot be reversed. It is an act of nature like being left handed. Lefties were born that way and cannot change. So it is with gays, many of whom feel privileged to be so oriented. So the term should be "sexual orientation."

The use of inappropriate language when referring to gays is abhorrent to them and they are trying to change this. Years ago, the words "fairy" and "queer" were used to describe a man who was considered homosexual. Some older people still persist in using these which offends the sensitive gay. There are certain expressions which grossly misrepresent and are particularly offensive to gays, one is that they are seeking special rights. They are only seeking the civil rights equal to those of straights.

Gays also object to being called "sodomites." Some heterosexuals practice sodomy. Are they not culprits as well? They also object to their sexual orientation being called a "sickness." There are people who believe this and that it can be cured. This is a totally false notion. Gays are as healthy as straights.

WHAT IS THE BOTTOM LINE?

Words that incorrectly identify gays in the media and in ordinary conversation serve to shape the public image, perceptions and even public policy, and these images become indelible in the minds of many people. For the first time in the history of our country, we are grappling with the role of gay and lesbians in our society, from the military to the workplace to the family, and gays and lesbians are trying to set the record straight.

Just what do gays and lesbians really want? All they want is to be considered as "people," just as straights are. Are they asking too much?

CHAPTER THREE
What Does Research Tell Us?

You must be wondering what the professionals think about homosexuals and if there has been research to find out why this occurs
in a percentage of the population. What makes a homosexual? It is
speculated that it is genetic or congenital or a combination of the
two. We are not sure which factor or how much of each is involved
or whether the environment plays a role as well.

Genetic implies a defective gene which has been present from
conception. Examples are mental retardation, Down's syndrome
and hemophilia, which are defects of a gene of one of the parents
and unchangeable once the sperm penetrates the ovum. Congenital
means that some influence during the baby's development within
the uterus interferes with normal formation. Examples are hare lip,
spina bifida, disintegration of the hip and other malformations of
the body.

HISTORY HAS NO ANSWERS

Recorded history points out that there is an incidence in the
population of male and female homosexuals and nothing that
happens during puberty or adolescence can prevent or change this.
Certain infants are stamped for life at birth with a brand of sexuality that is irreversible by the parents, the family, the environment,
training, peer pressure or other factor, including the individual
himself or herself. Sexual orientation, whether heterosexual or
homosexual or bisexual is derived from a prearranged direction set
in the baby's brain while in the uterus, triggered off at puberty but
usually evident earlier by behavior.

The theory that homosexuality is a product of the environment
is still widely held but has not been proved. In the late nineteenth
century this concept was firmly established in professional and lay
minds and it was believed that young boys could be made into
homosexuals by their mothers, by men or other boys. These concepts were formed from insufficient scientific evidence, reinforced

by superstition and pseudo science. Even today some psychiatrists claim heredity plays no part and that the environment or the mother can produce it and psychotherapy can remove it. None of this has been proved.

KINSEY WAS THE FIRST

Such beliefs were discredited by an extensive research project conducted at the Kinsey Institute for Sex Research at Indiana University. Fifteen hundred male and female homosexuals were interviewed after filling out a lengthy questionnaire. They testified that the parents had nothing to do with their sexual orientation and not one had become homosexual after a homosexual experience. It may be alleged that memories of childhood can be faulty, but until genetic engineering discovers the gene responsible, there is no research that challenges this study.

Kinsey and his team also conducted studies consisting of over five thousand men and five thousand women chosen at random from the general population and presumably heterosexual. Although these numbers are not necessarily representative of the population, they offer material for further study. Findings revealed that 37% of the men and 13% of the women had some homosexual experience to orgasm between adolescence and old age.

THE INCIDENCE IS ILLUSIVE

Don't we know how many heterosexuals, homosexuals and bisexuals there are in the population? No, we do not. The answer to this simple question has proven to be dubious, for the disapproval and rejection by society of the entire subject of sexual orientation has sent most gays into the closet, so how can one tell who is being honest when asked? Kinsey's research indicates a broad spectrum between the two extremes of heterosexuality and homosexuality, into which large numbers of individuals fall. But we don't know, nor does anyone, exactly what makes a person gay, straight of somewhere in between.

Homosexuality appears to run in families. Many gay men and women have a close relative who is also homosexual. Whether or not it crosses the sex line is not known, for instance, if a woman having a gay brother increases her chance of being gay, or vice versa.

So, a specific count of homosexuals at this point seems unlikely due to the unwillingness of many gays to admit their sexual orientation. Therefore, all we have to go on are the studies by Kinsey in 1948 to 1953, the first in this country, and studies by scientists in other countries before and after him. England's Havelock Ellis calculated that two to five percent of Englishmen were homosexual and Germany's Magnus Hirschfeld two percent. After Kinsey, further studies in this country and in England appear to corroborate his findings. However, the numbers can only be guessed at for Kinsey's were the first and so far, the last detailed studies.

One conclusion of the Kinsey report is that homosexual boys have unsatisfactory relationships with fathers who tend to be overbearing, controlling and lack understanding, the typical paranoid personality. Several psychiatrists have observed this over years of practice and, while still theoretical, it suggests a genetic influence on the fetus. The personality of the mother is less influential and little is known about her genetic or congenital effect, however, experiments with animals show that male homosexual activity shows up when the mother's hormonal balance is thrown off by adding male hormones. There is need for further study in this area.

Can homosexuality or the tendency thereof be detected in the brains of gay men and women? Yes, at autopsy, there is a difference in a part of the anterior hypothalamus that is two to three times larger in straight men than in women. In gay men, the same section is on average the same size as in straight women and two to three times smaller than in straight men. These are average differences. In simple terms, gay men don't have the type of brain cells that attracts them to women. Therefore, this research strengthens the notion that the brains of gay and straight men are different.

Following Kinsey, further studies indicate that some heterosexual men and women have isolated homosexual experiences at some time in their lives, but it does not influence their inherent heterosexual orientation.

Nature has a strange way of fooling us and one is the determination of sex. Is the unborn baby male or female? How is this decided? Can we control it? No, we cannot. It is claimed that the sperm determines the sex of the fetus but how and why? Some families have five girls and one boy, others more boys than girls, yet the ratio of male to female babies remains fairly constant at a hundred and seven boys to a hundred girls, a number of which are homosexual, which also appears to remain stable.

WE ALL BEGIN AS AN EMBRYO

Every embryo within the womb, after it has been fertilized by a spermatozoa, starts out as a female. In a little over one half of cases a message is sent, whose nature is unknown, which results in the above ratio being born in the general population. The sex chromosomes are called X and Y, both of which men have. Women have only a Y. An individual's sex is determined by the gene TDF (testis determining factor) located on the Y chromosome, causing the development of a male. In order to effect this, the gene TDF is turned on after several obscure maneuvers, otherwise all fetuses would be female. Thus, a fixed proportion of embryos become male.

Do genes determine sexual orientation or does the environment play a role? Is it a combination of the two or what? This is an exceedingly controversial question but recent studies of twins and adoptive siblings point toward a large genetic factor that is involved in the etiology of homosexuality. These studies at the National Institutes of Health link some instances of homosexuality to a small area of DNA on chromosome X. If this can be confirmed, it may lead to a better understanding of sexual orientation in general.

Now scientists are looking for a homosexuality gene through family histories. They find that brothers of homosexuals are more likely to be homosexual than men in the general population. It is interesting that the majority of gays seem to come from the maternal side of the family, which implies that for some gay males the trait is passed through the mother. Information from family histories indicates that there are more homosexual relatives on the maternal side than on the paternal side and it is more common among maternal uncles of gay men and cousins who are sons of maternal aunts than among males in the general population.

This implies that at least for some homosexuals the trait is passed through the female, so the place to look for the gene is the X chromosome, the only one inherited from the mother. Finally, it was found that near the end of the long arm of the X chromosome there is a set of five markers that is shared by the homosexuals in the group of the men studied and not by the heterosexuals.

Scientists warn, however, that this does not explain all male homosexuality because the research turned up instances where the trait was passed on paternally. Therefore, it may be that homosexuality occurs from several causes. Once the gene is identified much more can be learned.

THERE ARE OTHER FORMS OF SEXUALITY

So, in addition to homosexuals, nature gives us more categories of sexual orientation, the ambisexuals described in chapter I, the number of which is unknown, and an extremely small group that is neither male or female, the hermaphrodites. The word comes from the Greek god Hermes, the messenger and patron of music, and Aphrodite, the goddess of sexual love and beauty. Greek mythology tells us that these two gods parented Hermaphroditus, who fell in love at fifteen with a nymph, fused his body with hers and became half male and half female.

In medical terms, hermaphrodites are described as having intersexual bodies, so the term "intersex" is used as a catch-all for three subgroups that have a mixture of one kind or other of male and female characteristics. The true hermaphrodites, called "herms," have one testis and one ovary. There are male pseudohermaphrodites who have two testes and some aspect of female genitalia but no ovaries, called "merms," and the female counterpart with ovaries and some aspect of the male genitalia but no testes are the "ferms." These are physiological determinations but the sub-groups are very complex within themselves, each varying widely in emotional and psychological aspects. It is speculated that these three intersexes, herm, merm and ferm should be considered sexes in their own right, therefore, with the usual male and female, there may even be more than five sexes. However, the incidence of the intersexuals is unknown, but it is guessed that they are about four percent of all births.

DOES THIS OCCUR IN ANIMALS?

If the human race has always had homosexuals in some degree of the population, what about other mammals, such as monkeys and apes? Actually, according to Kinsey, homosexual contacts occur in practically every species and this has been extensively studied and occurs fairly frequently, although not as frequently as heterosexual activity. This may be because the characteristic submissiveness of the female and aggressiveness of the male permit insertion into the vagina more easily than into the male anus. The motivating factor is the primitive urge for sexual satisfaction.

It can be hypothesized that the fundamental cause of homosexuality in humans is a result of the remaining vestige of the evolutionary process of searching for the ultimate goal of perpetuating the species, which is the primary objective of the sex drive. In other words, the innate aggressiveness of the male was put there for this purpose, and in seeking a mate back in evolutionary history he was driven to find "somewhere to put it" and, at times lacking a female, found another male. Regarding female animals, they are less aggressive than males but the urge to perpetuate the species also prevails in them, so they seek the submissive target of other females.

RESEARCH IS ONGOING

So just what does research tell us about homosexuality? Unfortunately, nothing specific as to why there are homosexuals and how they become that way, however, the sum of it all makes it clear that heterosexual and homosexual orientations are not exclusively and always strictly one or the other. There is a great deal of theorizing and speculation, however, and many studies have been done and many are ongoing, but none so far gives us definitive answers.

Nevertheless, we have learned from this work facts that appear to be irrefutable, that a certain percentage of males and females are born homosexual, that they did not choose and cannot change it. Furthermore, we have learned that there are several variations of homosexuality in both men and women. But there are many questions that remain unanswered, such as the etiology or cause, is the condition inherited, does the environment play a part and why, when one identical twin is homosexual in fifty percent of cases, the other is not?

THERE ARE DIFFERENCES IN THE BRAIN

What do these studies prove? Nothing conclusive but they indicate possible avenues of research to pursue in order to come closer to the answers we are looking for. For instance, a recent study in Canada hypothesizes that there is a neurobiological basis for sexual orientation based on the anatomical differences in the brains of homosexuals. This points to a strong genetic role and the fact that there is a link between homosexuality and left-handedness. Further research suggests and is already confirmed by other studies that homosexuals were exposed to unusual levels of sex hormones prenatally. It is the belief that evidence from several sources suggests that sexual orientation is part of a larger constellation of cognitive attributes, which may explain the prevalence of homosexual over heterosexual men in some professions as well as their high aptitude in these disciplines.

Recently, a renowned neurobiologist identified a tiny but important difference between the brains of homosexual and heterosexual men in the part of the hypothalamus that influences sexual behavior. As mentioned earlier, it is a spot half the size in homosexuals as in heterosexuals and about the same size as in women. Two questions remain, however, does this difference cause homosexuality, and if so, what caused it to develop and when? At about the same time, another scientist discovered another difference in the brain. There is a small bridge that connects the two brain hemispheres that is larger in females than in males and the larger bridge is also in gay men. The causes and reasons are unknown, but there is much speculation.

Identical male twins from three groups were studied. Fifty-six pairs were identical, sharing the same genes, fifty-four pairs were fraternal, sharing half the same genes, and fifty-seven pairs of adoptive brothers who don't share any genes. Homosexuality occurred in fifty-two percent of both brothers in the first group of identical twins, in twenty-two percent of both fraternal twins and eleven percent of adoptive brothers. This study highlights the probability that genes play a role in the determination of homosexuality and subsequently, similar studies on lesbian women produced identical results, all of which points to a strong genetic component in the etiology of homosexuality. The answer to when and how, however, remains unknown.

So far we have discussed research on gay men. What about the lesbians? There is a study on twins in women using the same types of twins as in men and showing the identical result, i.e., a strong genetic influence. So it is hypothesized that genes play an important role in shaping sexual orientation, although no specific gene or genes are identified.

Recently, there has been a breakthrough in regard to the cause of some cases of male homosexuality. Researchers have identified a gene lying on a small section of the X chromosome inherited by men from their mothers that contributes to their sexual orientation. Although the gene is not yet identified, it is speculated that it may perform functions linked to sexuality. However, these data must be replicated and if they are confirmed, it will be the first gene linked to a high level function performed by the healthy human brain.

This new evidence hopefully may herald the ability of scientists to study the brain in the process of thinking, observing sexual impulses and determining how the heterosexual and the homosexual differ. After all, it is the workings of the brain that define sexual function, not the ovaries and the gonads.

OTHER ISSUES ARE INVOLVED
The possibility that a gene underlies a type of homosexuality brings up social, ethical and political issues. If these findings are confirmed, it would be possible to test unborn babies and/or men and this would enter into moral, ethical and political issues, such as gays in the military, the question of abortion and discrimination against gays who prefer to remain in the closet and have had to submit to testing.

There is still controversy as to whether or not the environment plays a role, small though it may be, but just enough to push the gene responsible over the edge. This work, which is being done in Germany, shows that during World War II more homosexuals were born than in peace time. It is speculated that stress to the mother during pregnancy may have been a factor. On the other hand, there is strong evidence that a homosexual parent does not play a part in producing a gay man or woman.

LET US SPECULATE

Assume that we accept the premise that genes play a role in the development of homosexuality. In other words, that there is an inherited factor. The question of when this occurs and how it takes place is a mystery. A possible explanation is the male and female sex hormones, for in many species of animals they affect the manner in which the brain is formed, thus influencing the determination of gender and its various manifestations.

Finally, it is evident that in order to find out why some men and women are born homosexual, a next logical approach is to determine the gene or genes responsible.

We emphasize that what determines heterosexuality, bisexuality and homosexuality is largely unknown. However, there are indications that sexual orientation is strongly influenced by happenings during the developmental stage of the fetus when the brain is under the influence of gonadal steroids. The genes also play a considerable role, and the environment also, both prenatally and after birth, such as through stress of the mother, interactions within the family and social and sexual influences during adolescence and early adulthood. Much more will be learned through study of the genes and their affects on sexuality.

CHAPTER FOUR
If Gays Want To Change, Can They?

Do gays want to change? No, not really, but the adverse pressures of the world they live in makes it almost impossible to resist trying to change, and many have wanted to in order to be the same as the heterosexual, primarily because they know they are "different" and want to be like everybody else. Then, as they grow older, they are besieged by family, friends and peers at school and church, and the enormous pressure becomes so great that many gays seek some means of changing their sexual identity "to be cured."

HOMOSEXUALITY IS NOT A SICKNESS

The word "cure" implies sickness and to be homosexual is not being sick. As I've mentioned many times, gays have grown up and remain surrounded by a culture that regards homosexuality as sick or a wicked way to be and against God's will. These concepts are absolutely false as I've already stated. Gays who have asked to have their sexual orientation changed as a last desperate grab for acceptance by the straight world, have without exception come to deeply regret that decision. This pressure by society to force gays to change puts a burden on them that has never been visited upon straights. This is unfortunate, for the emotional and psychological havoc that such a program produces is devastating beyond description and can wreak irreparable damage.

Ask any gay person if he or she is "sick" and the answer is always an emphatic "No, I don't feel sick, I like it the way I am and I don't want to even think of trying to change." However, there are times when the gay male does not feel that No is the answer because of the negative effects of the social environment upon his psyche. This impels him to consider the possibility of changing in order to be relieved of the lonely and painful existence of being in the silent ghetto.

Moreover, in making a decision, the gay male is unduly conscious of his many friends who have been taught that they are sick and, having come to believe it, often succumb to self-destruction through suicide or drug abuse. So the decision is an ominous one. All this talk results in straight people suspecting that gays are trying to convert straights to their homosexual orientation. However, it is the other way around. It is the straights who are trying to convert gays, and with the loftiest of intentions, believing that they are sick and unhappy and want to be like us.

AN ATTEMPT TO BE "CURED" CAN BE DISASTROUS

It is unfortunate that the words "sickness" and "curing" have become common usage when referring to gay people. The proper term is "behavior modification," and this is what is attempted by those gays who are driven to try to change.

There is the story of a man who went through every conceivable "cure," none of which worked. Still adamant to try everything, he submitted himself to an "exorcism" to drive out the "gay demon." This exercise convinced him that he was "cured," but after a few months, the gay feelings surfaced and he went into an hysterical panic, crying over and over "I am evil, evil, and even God cannot cure me!" He was a priest, and it took months of psychotherapy to convince him that he was not evil.

So this is what happens to gays who are coerced by others wanting to help or by their own volition to change to heterosexuality.

As already explained, homosexuality occurs naturally in a percentage of men and women and for the most part is irreversible, although there are rare exceptions in the form of several variations that emanated from the Kinsey studies of individuals who knew they were different but did not know why. Also, there are others with a low sex drive and no interest in sex, and some of the bisexual group who vacillate between homosexual and heterosexual behavior before finally adhering to a same sex preference.

WHY DO STRAIGHTS WANT GAYS TO CHANGE?

It seems that compassion for a gay person by a straight is

nothing more than a desire to change him or her and some people attempt to do just that. Few straights either don't know or will not admit that this is not possible and persist in efforts to persuade gays to change.

Why do straights want gays to change? Many, in good conscience, feel sorry for them and want to help them become "normal" human beings. Some parents cannot face the fact that their child is "dirty," and feel that they are tainted as well. There are siblings who fear that having a homosexual brother or sister will make others think that they are all gay or that it can even affect their chances of getting along in life. These erroneous concepts can cause unbelievable anguish, so a gay may often look for help to change out of desperation.

This is the experience of one gay who knew that he was gay since a small child. Let's call him Simon. While in college, where he was surrounded by his peers, all of whom in his dorm were straight, he was tempted to be like the others and change his sexual orientation. His teacher was the centerfold in the current Playboy Magazine which had been floating about the dormitory exciting the students. Simon decided to give it a whirl just to see if it would work and found it curious that he also became aroused when his roommate gushed over the sensuous picture.

So he went to work in private. Simon was eighteen and a virgin, and although he had always had fantasies about men, he had never had a sexual experience except for self- masturbation. At this point, however, he made a valiant attempt to switch his desires to the luscious lady in the magazine and practiced assiduously to do so.

This went on for four months and for a time Simon thought it was working and that he could respond sexually to a female. He wanted this mostly because he felt that being heterosexual like most men is the way to go. He also wanted desperately to be accepted into the mainstream of society and live no longer in the constant dread of discovery. But to no avail. Simon finally had to accept the fact that he simply could not change, so he relaxed, stopped the striving and retreated into his normal, innate self of being homosexual.

THE MASTERS AND JOHNSON PROGRAM

"Change" or "cure" programs are referred to by Masters and Johnson as "conversion" or "reversion" treatment and were sought out by both gay men and lesbians, more men than women. The term conversion applies to men and women who have never had a heterosexual experience, and reversion to those who had or were married, and had become less and less able to have sexual intercourse with their wives or husbands. The degree of motivation of the client was important in evaluating the method of treatment and the chance of success. While a relatively few homosexuals asked to have their sexual orientation changed, the motivating reason of all was because of societal rejection and business pressures. None expressed a real desire.

In the Masters and Johnson study of gays and lesbians, some requested conversion to heterosexuality, and others wanted to be reverted to the sexual activity they enjoyed in younger days. The method required that the patient be treated with a person of the opposite sex, as one on one therapy did not appear to be as successful. Each case was studied thoroughly and the treatment outlined and altered along the way as circumstances warranted. The results were mixed. Some patients returned to homosexuality, some became or remained ambivalent, and most decided for reversion or conversion and maintained their commitment over the ten years after treatment, during which time they were followed up. Eleven men and three women failed the treatment, sixteen men and three women were lost to follow-up. The overall failure rate was twenty-eight percent.

Here are the detailed results of the study. Eleven males opted for conversion and two failed. Forty-five were treated for reversion and nine failed. Thirteen lesbians were treated for conversion and three failed, and three treated for conversion and none failed. These small numbers should not be considered as an indication of what the results would be in a larger program. All those who failed returned to homosexuality.

The devastating depression that ensues after an unsuccessful attempt at conversion or reversion is tragic to observe. Such a depression is extremely difficult to treat.

Notwithstanding, Masters and Johnson relate several cases of bisexual males who have reverted totally to heterosexuality with the fervent assistance of their wives, resulting in a compatible and happy marriage with children and harmony. However, these histories date back to the middle 1970s and as far as we know there has been no follow-up. These are isolated cases that have turned out well, but they are rare. Reversion therapy has seldom been successful when encouraged and induced by a spouse or when the individual expressed a desire to continue a homosexual relationship and not accept complete conversion.

WHY WOULD A GAY WANT TO CHANGE?

For what reason would a gay man want to revert? There are several. Some gays fall in love with a woman and marry, but as the years go on, and the revulsion of heterosexual contact begins to erode the sexual life of the couple, the gay spouse can no longer tolerate the situation and takes a same-sex lover. The heterosexual mate is left high and dry and a frank discussion between the two culminates in a desire to revert.

What is the consensus today in regard to changing? Most gays have no desire to change, the straight community continues as it always has and the medical profession has finally thrown in the towel and admits that change is not possible and no longer believes that homosexuals, willing or not, must be persuaded to submit to a regimen that will change them. It is clear that efforts to this effect have drastically altered their thinking.

Over the years, many techniques, some even barbaric, have been employed in order to change sexual orientation. Examples are the introduction of needles into the brain, the transplantation of testicles of heterosexual males into the homosexual, and the injection of hormones. Psychoanalysis and aversion therapy have been tried, and electric shock. Gentler versions of therapy are behavior modification, desensitization, sensitization and conditioning techniques. All have been tried and all have failed.

Ask any homosexual, male or female, if he or she wants to change. The answer is always no. Ask them if they would have preferred to have been born straight. The answer is yes.

CHAPTER FIVE
The Life of the Gay

WHAT IS IT LIKE TO BE A GAY MAN?

Early in life he realizes that he is different from the other boys. He feels isolated from the others and very much alone, no one to share feelings with. So he removes himself from the world he was born in and into the silent ghetto where he feels totally alone, until one day he discovers that he is not alone any more and thanks God.

He was taught from childhood that the world does not condone homosexuality and that it is an unmentionable of decent people. He is told that homosexuals are perverted, vile, evil and God hates them. Yet he is surrounded by family and friends who say they love him, not knowing the truth, and all the time reiterating how they hate faggots and fairies and dykes. So he encloses himself even more tightly into the silent ghetto for fear of being discovered.

As time goes on and he grows up, he discovers that there are hundreds of millions just like him, all confined to that silent ghetto and the straights looking down upon them. You wonder what they would do if they knew that they are living next to and working with and consorting socially with one of us. Even a brother or sister may be gay and he doesn't know it, for this ghetto has no physical boundaries. Within it are people of every nation, creed, ethnic, political and economic origin and all are forbidden to mention that they are gay.

He looks around and sees what happens to those who do break out of the ghetto and speak out. He sees gays turned out of their neighborhoods, some disowned by their parents. He sees his gay brothers and sisters turning to drugs, alcohol or suicide as a way out. So for protection, he remains silent. This is the silent ghetto.

AND LIFE GOES ON

The gay man awakens in the morning and goes about his daily activities much as everyone else, except for one respect. He must be constantly alert to the fact that he is gay and different from most men and has to be always fearful of discovery and never let his guard down. Some gays come out of the closet early, but they usually find a hostile world and learn to live in an unwelcome and uncomfortable environment. Some choose a field of work where they are apt to meet other gays and where the milieu is conducive to acceptance. But in the world at large, they must be wary.

HIS PEERS CAN BE CRUEL

It is unfortunate that young boys must have a macho image in order to be accepted by the peer group. What most people don't know is that the delicate-looking boy is not necessarily homosexual, in fact, most such boys are straight but they, along with the effeminate gays, take a beating by the other boys. This goes as well for the girls who are tomboys. All girls are supposed to be pretty, feminine and should dress accordingly, but how many really fit that model?

There are girls who are into sports and like to dress in pants and there are men who are sensitive and artistic and adopt the gentler ways of women. Most are straight. Any mature individual who has a modicum of self esteem, gay or straight, will act like him or herself, regardless of what others say or think. For that is how God made them.

There are many talented gays who contribute more to society than the average straight. Some are famous in the field of the dance, painting, music, writing and fashion design. They tend to have in-born aesthetic and artistic skills, which they are more apt to develop than straight individuals, who are principally occupied with family and making a living. Over the centuries, enormous contributions have been made by homosexuals such as Plato and Michelangelo.

HOW DOES A GAY FEEL?

After accepting the fact that he is homosexual, he runs the gamut of emotions, from being ashamed that he is different from most others, he may be angry and think he is sick, he may feel guilty and put himself down, he may be humiliated and ashamed. The persistent turmoil and self-hate are desolating. Finally for most, acceptance of himself as he is takes over.

DO GAY MEN HAVE ANY FUN?

How does a gay man spend his leisure time? He may go "cruising," a term also applied to straights when they frequent bars and social gatherings where they can meet people. We hear about "gay" bars and wonder what they are like. Some are like any other bar, a place to meet people, talk, drink and maybe dance. Others cater to particular interests of the customers, such as an older age group, drugs, baths, massage and sauna rooms, jacuzzis and particularly the availability of anonymous sex without having to become involved.

Just as a young straight man goes about looking for a girl to whom he is attracted, so does the gay look for a man. It could be a woman or a man in the case of a bisexual. Occasionally, a gay may make a mistake and think a man is gay when he is not, and this is like walking into a hornet's nest, for the straight immediately recoils at the slightest indication of being taken for a homosexual.

The reaction of a straight male to this may be severe and he may lose control and assault a gay. Depending on personality, a straight feels justified in his behavior, even if it leads to violence. The sensitivity of a heterosexual male to a homosexual is so strong that he feels no compunction about exerting violent behavior.

In addition, there are the want ads in the newspaper. At times a gay man or woman may not want to seek a partner in a public place, so the want ad is the way to go. Just pick up a local newspaper and you will find a plethora of opportunities. There are numerous ads under "Men Seeking Men" and "Women Seeking Women," one is entitled "Entre Nous," and another "Part Time Love," all directed to bisexuals of either sex. And for the gay man, there are gay prostitutes who frequent the streets just as members of the "oldest" profession do. They are attractive, handsome and well dressed. They are careful not to perform or allow sexual activities that jeopardize the health of either party. Some make good friends with their clients and become long term lovers. The married bisexual often relies on them for sexual satisfaction.

THE SEX LIFE OF THE GAY MALE

The gay male is interested in new experiences. He is out for the pleasure of the moment and eager to try anything different. The more doing type leads a grasshopper life, has many partners and a variety of activities. If he has a satisfying orgasm, he doesn't worry about anything else. There are no lasting bonds and no concern for his partner. However, life is not easy for him for he has to develop a life-style that accommodates his sexual tendencies, and sooner or later he collides with a social, psychological or physical problem to cope with, essentially alone.

The more thinking type of individual is apt to want to settle down to a more lasting relationship with someone of the same inclination. Although they may continue to live together, their sexual relationship is usually short lived. They might change lovers frequently even while sharing the same quarters, for loyalty is sometimes limited. This is not true of all gays, however, some of whom establish strong relationships that start out as sexual liaisons and evolve into solid friendships with no sexual activity. This may last a lifetime.

THE NATURE OF THE SEX DRIVE

As in all people, straight and gay, the sex drive ranges from low to high and personality traits also play a part in their sexual activity as to choice of partner, frequency of sexual contacts and type of behavior. The straight community has the impression that all gays are extremely promiscuous and spend a great deal of time searching for sex partners but this is not necessarily true. Such an impression emanates from media descriptions of high drive men.

A case in point is that of an airline steward who was gay. His job took him all over the world and at every layover he would pick up a "trick" or two. Along the way he became HIV positive and eventually developed AIDS, but carried on as long as he could with his job and his philandering. When he became very ill he confessed to his sexual contacts and several cases of AIDS in cities where he had been were traced to him.

The sexual drive in the male, both straight and gay, is an animalistic one and much stronger and more vigorous than that of the female. Most men get so caught up in their sexual needs that they acquire a "don't care" attitude and may become careless.

However, there are isolated instances of what is called "situational homosexuality" that occur under circumstances when there is no other outlet for the sexual drive. This is frequently exhibited by men and women confined for a long period with members of their own sex, such as on ship board or in prison. Upon release, they resume their usual sexual behavior.

Moreover, for the most part the homosexual population is more educated than the heterosexual population and they feel deprived of their rights because they are not accepted, so they tend to be more cautious about their sexual activity.

It is the impression of scientists and lay people alike that male gays have an unusually high frequency of sexual outlets. Studies by Kinsey and his team refute this and indicate that the frequency is not out of line with the average male straight and, in fact, the number of outlets of the homosexual male is lower per week than that of the married heterosexual male.

WHAT ABOUT THE LESBIAN?

What does that word mean and why are homosexual women called lesbians? The word comes from the Greek island of Lesbos, on which Sappho lived. She was reputed to love women instead of men, hence the term lesbian, and "sapphic," taken from her name, is also used. Thus, female homosexuals are usually referred to as lesbians. They are greatly out numbered by male homosexuals for reasons unknown, although the ratio between them has never been established. A guess would be two to one. It is known, however, from studies by the Kinsey laboratory, that the origin of female homosexuality is the same as that of males.

The sexual drive of women is not as strong as that of men and Kinsey's studies confirm this. However, long term commitment among lesbian couples greatly out numbers those of male gays, which are rare. Furthermore, the studies show that over fifty percent of lesbians had only one partner and twenty percent had two, only four percent had ten or more. So the lesbian far outdoes the gay man in constancy.

There are bisexual lesbians as there are bisexual males, and a gay woman may have an affair with a man coincidentally or from time to time during her lifetime, whether she is married or single.

LESBIANS HAVE BEEN DISREGARDED

From ancient history on, much emphasis has been placed on facilities and institutions for men and for male gays. There have always been taverns, public baths, gymnasia and so forth, but never at any time in history has anything of that sort been established for lesbians. This discrepancy is based on the psychosexual differences between the two sexes, the lower female sex drive and the age old assumption that women are inferior to men.

As with the male gay, the lesbian suffers the same discrimination and fear of discovery, but to a lesser extent, mostly because of appearances. However, if a lesbian chooses to dress in mannish clothes, this may cause her to be suspect. In addition, there is the age old problem of the parents who reject their daughter upon learning that she is homosexual, as well as siblings and close friends who do not understand.

DO GAY MALES AND LESBIANS GET TOGETHER?

Formerly, male and female homosexuals did not associate on a regular basis, but this has changed gradually in the last twenty years. Although gay men don't visit bars frequented by lesbians, and lesbians don't visit gay male hangouts, they enjoy one another's company at parties and get togethers when both gay sexes are united, and in a gay parade or festival, where the mixing is free and easy. Furthermore, in many southwestern and southern cities there are bars in the gay districts, usually discos, that are known for the gay male and female clientele, and leaders of both groups join in an effort to eradicate any dichotomy that may exist. Moreover, gay men and women are getting to know one another more and more on a friendly and personal basis and often become fast friends.

THE SEXUAL ROLES OF GAY COUPLES

There is a great deal of confusion among straights about the male and female roles of gay couples. They seem to be convinced that one of a couple has to be female and the other male. This is not the case. A gay couple has no concern for husband and wife roles that define the duties in a straight marriage. They are simply two men or two women, each with his or her own career who are deeply in love with one another and have made a commitment to spend their lives together in mutual love, emotionally, spiritually, intellectually and sexually.

Straights assume that gay men cast themselves in the role of the male or female partner and that one is the man and the other the woman. This is not so, although a few couples assume one role or the other and may change back and forth. Sometimes the female role includes the household duties of a women and the receptor in anal intercourse. However, for the majority of gays, male and female, taking turns is the usual norm.

Some gay men are effeminate in their general behavior and prefer the receptive role in anal intercourse and there are some who are macho/straight and always take the insertive role. A large group of gays have no preference for one or the other and freely interchange roles with all partners. Furthermore, there are many practices that don't involve masculine and feminine roles.

WHAT DOES THE GAY MAN DO IN BED?

What can they do, two men together? The answer is the same as what a straight couple does. They hug and kiss and fondle one another. The only difference is that there is no penis/vagina penetration, but some gay males substitute anal intercourse. Not all gay men practice this and it is potentially harmful to the partner. The anus is not designed to accommodate an erect penis and stretching the sphincter muscle can cause pain and serious damage, such as hemorrhoids and/or rupture. This may result in fecal incontinence and carries the danger of infection for both parties.

A more common practice is mutual manipulation of the penis, another is oral intercourse (fellatio), which is sometimes reciprocated, sometimes not. Today, many gays are rejecting anal intercourse in favor of masturbation and oral sex, because the anal route is not only a dangerous practice but because of the fear of AIDS. It is the most effective sexual means for spreading the AIDS virus. This applies to straights as well as gays for some straights also engage in anal intercourse.

AND LESBIANS?

The most common sexual activity of lesbians is mutual masturbation to orgasm by manipulating the clitoris. Alternately, the lesbian inserts one finger into the vagina and caresses the anus with
another, while stroking the clitoris with a third. Oral stimulation is
also common. Mutual clitoral stimulation is also seen among anthro-
poid apes, which suggests that lesbian and gay male sex as well as
male/female sexuality predate the evolution of the human species.

Partners may use the American position, woman on woman,
and come to orgasm by rubbing the genitals together. The roles are
interchangeable. Vibrators are used frequently and cunnilingus,
(stimulation of the clitoris with the tongue) is common. Artificial
penises made of rubber or plastic can be strapped to the body to
simulate a male penis.

While the male homosexual focuses on the penis, with erection
and orgasm his goal, this is not the case with lesbians. Their sexual
encounters are longer, and an important part involves kissing, hug-
ging, and caressing one another. Their lovemaking reflects a woman's
search for affection and love, as opposed to the largely physical sex
act of the male.

There are bisexual women, but the number is small, and as with
men, the dominant drive takes precedence as time goes on. Marriages with men are scarce, but they do occur and tend to last longer than those of male bisexuals. As they grow older, these women
seem able to handle marriage, children and a lesbian relationship
comfortably.

HOW DO YOU COME OUT?

Regardless of the negatives, the decision has been made to
come out, so how does one start? Here is a hypothetical case. What
you do first is to tell the family and close friends. Don't be afraid,
they may have already suspected. Once this is done, the word will
soon be out for all to know. You have accomplished an act of important emotional and psychological consequences and it may turn
your life around.

This has not been easy. The hardest part was making up your
mind and now that you have taken that leap you will be a happier

person, you can meet your own kind, make friends and get on with your life.

This is how one gay handled it. "When I came out of the closet at age twenty-nine, I had a difficult time convincing my friends that I really was gay. I had always been regarded as a butch type and it never entered their heads that such a type could be homosexual. I had already told my parents and they accepted me. Occasionally, the subject of homosexuality would come up with their friends usually in a negative vein, critical and derogatory. My mother would gently take offense and say: 'Yes, my son is gay, but he is a normal gay.'"

Another gay friend told me: "When I finally decided to come out of the closet, I wanted to celebrate, so I staged a coming out party like some young women have when they reach eighteen. I never had any desire to wear women's clothes, but this time I was determined to make it a howling success to be remembered by all who attended. I wore a fake diamond tiara on a blond wig and a pink tutu, actually two of them so they would reach around my ample girth, and a T-shirt with a picture on it of the wicked witch from the Wizard of OZ. I had a wedding cake with a tiny girl on the top, dressed in pink. I gave party favors to the guests, lavender ribbons for the men's hair and cigars for the women. The party was a smashing success and we all had a wonderful time. I was in drag for the first and undoubtedly the last time in my life."

WHAT IS "DRAG"?

Drag is when a male gay dresses in a woman's clothes and emulates one, swinging his hips and flirting in an exaggerated fashion. Some homosexuals look down upon drag as much as straights and condemn its use, but why do some gays who are not in drag appear to flaunt their homosexuality? Occasionally, you see an effeminate man swish by with limp wrists and swaying hips, only to be followed by remarks such as, "You would think he had more sense than to act that way!" The fact is that he is not acting. He knows no other way, and is simply being himself. It is the same with the masculine acting lesbian.

This is the way one gay described his situation. He was a real "drag queen" and had become deeply involved in the activist movement for equal civil rights for gays. He was exceedingly effeminate and, when asked why he became so involved when his mere appearance incited dislike and opposition among straights, he replied, smiling: "Honey, when you are six foot six like I am, have a lisp, a swishy walk and an insatiable desire for chiffon evening dresses, you might as well stand up and be counted, for people are going to notice you even if you are sitting down!"

THE HEALTH OF THE GAY MALE

Diseases that are sexually transmitted by gays are bacterial and viral in nature. Some are precancerous and passed around so rapidly that they create a high percentage of incidence. This is not a health threat to the public except through the bisexual married man who goes into the city for a gay weekend and might take an infection back to his wife. A woman is more health conscious than most men and seeks medical attention more readily and sees that her husband does too.

Sexual activity involving the anus and rectum presents a health hazard that is becoming increasingly serious. Not only is there a rising incidence of the common infections which have always plagued gay males, but AIDS is insidious. AIDS depletes the immune system and lays it open to many disorders, including a cancer called Kaposi's sarcoma and a previously unknown type of pneumonia, incurable so far.

It is true that the highest incidence of AIDS appeared to emanate from the gay male population when the HIV infection was first identified in 1981. Once the method of its transfer from person to person was discovered, however, no segment of society has made greater strides than the gay male population. Since the 1970s, when gay men engaged in sex with almost every gay male they knew, matters have changed dramatically. The incidence of infection dropped fast and continues to drop, and is rising among heterosexuals and IV drug users and teenagers, most of whom are straight.

So male homosexuality presents hazards. As gays circulate from one encounter to the next, an infected man comes into contact with others and spreads disease. Thus, reservoirs of infection are established and are extremely difficult to eradicate. The tragedy is that while most conditions are amenable to treatment, the gay doesn't go for it soon enough and often arrives at the doctor's office too late. As a matter of fact, all men, gay and straight alike, have a tendency to ignore illness or the possibility of illness. Any doctor will admit that men don't pay attention to their health until they get really sick or have a bad pain or injury. They also tend to ignore preventive measures that maintain health.

PERSONALITY PLAYS A PART

Gays function in different ways depending on personality. The extreme doer picks up a partner anywhere. He exchanges sexual advances in men's washrooms, on the street, or at the baths. The man he picks up is likely to be of the same type.

The more thinking gay doesn't participate in casual sex. He finds a partner through social channels and is apt to maintain the relationship longer. He is more conservative about admitting his sexual orientation but is not ashamed of it nor is it his temperament to flaunt it. He makes the rounds of social circles without being recognized as homosexual and engages in few frivolous sexual excesses. The gay relationships he forms are healthy and caring and he has respect for his partners and treats them in a loving and affectionate manner.

WHAT IS A TRANSVESTITE?

Queens are not to be confused with "transvestites," (literally—"cross dressers"). Transvestism is the impulse to dress in the clothing of the opposite sex in order to derive sexual satisfaction. In some cases, a man may take an article of his wife's or lover's clothing and touch his genitals. This is a stimulant to arousal and is usually a prelude to intercourse or, more often, to masturbation.

Transvestism is a genetic trait that remains throughout life. It is rare and extremely rare in women. It is a recessive gene that crops up with no known family history and is a wiring defect in the brain whereby the stimulation that usually comes from a woman or a man comes instead from that person's clothing. It is not serious and should be accepted as a minor sexual variation with no harmful effects. It seldom presents a problem except when there are feelings of guilt or disapproval through lack of understanding by the spouse.

Male transvestites are normal, heterosexual males who marry, have children and make good husbands and fathers. When they want to give in to this compulsion, they dress behind closed doors in feminine apparel, which arouses them to a degree they can reach no other way and allows them to be more passionate with their wives. Transvestites are not homosexuals, although homosexuals are as prone to inherit the gene as the heterosexual, but as already stated, it is a rare condition. Some people contend that only homosexuals are transvestites because some dress in drag, but this assertion is false. Transvestism is separate and distinct from homosexuality and is found predominately among heterosexuals. The same percentage of gays are transvestites as are straights, but there are about nine times as many straights as gays in the world.

WHAT BRINGS ABOUT A MAN'S SEXUAL DESIRE?

It is interesting to be aware of the various stimuli that arouse a man, whether he be heterosexual or homosexual. Female nudity, a woman's breasts or shapely legs are the usual enticers for most men but there are others that are rather uncommon, such as those required by the transvestite and the fetisher, and there are other unusual stimuli such as being whipped or spanked that are required in order to excite some men and allow them to have intercourse.

Aside from what arouses him, variety seems to be more important to homosexual than to heterosexual men, although both may have the same impulse. Despite a good marriage, husbands often have fantasies about other women, but when a homosexual fantasizes, he usually takes action to find a new relationship. On the other hand, how many married men are monogamous? To our knowledge, there has never been a study to determine this, nor the monogamous incidence of women. It is common knowledge that "hanky-panky" is a way of life for some men and probably some women, for it takes two to tango.

Some homosexuals hold that the admitted promiscuity of gays is due to the abuse, rejection and lack of respect to which they are subjected, and if this were removed and they had available the civil and legal rights of heterosexuals, this would be drastically reduced. The present trend, although slow, is in this direction.

THE LIFE OF THE BISEXUAL MALE

A large group of men are bisexual, and have considerable experience with both men and women. Both influences are strong and a man is capable of failing in love with a woman or a man, and his choice of a partner may be almost by chance. He may marry and have children but if he is at a young age when his sex drive is high, he can channel some into his marriage, at least for a time. However, as he grows older, he cannot keep pace with the sexual demands of both wife and lover, and the weaker drive falters. In addition, he is apt to become disillusioned as the children grow into adolescence, family conflicts arise and the implications of his life-style hit home. Furthermore, he may be having difficulty achieving an erection and orgasm with his wife which is apt to happen as he reaches middle age.

As the sexual drive diminishes, he turns to the easiest stimulation, the homosexual, because that is what he basically responds to and enjoys most. Then he is likely to leave his wife for a calmer life with his lover.

How does the wife feel? She is upset and feels at fault, reasoning that if she had been a better wife she could have kept him. Even though she blames herself, she feels cheated, and this makes her angry. The fault, if any, lies in marrying him knowing he was bisexual, if indeed she did know, and believing she could solidify their relationship by being a good and loving wife and having children, or perhaps she did not know that he was gay because he never told her. And how many women know you cannot change a bisexual into a heterosexual? Some wives believe they can and try but to no avail.

Sometimes these marriages last, but it is rare. If the wife is aware of her husband's proclivity and is tolerant of it, she may want to keep the marriage together for the sake of the children, his business and social reasons. She has little sex life with her husband, however, and may have affairs or abstain from sex.

A common belief is that bisexuals marry to hide their sexual orientation, but this is not true. It is usually because they fall in love. If they have children, they are very attached to them and make good fathers, and are often able to cope with them better than their wives. They may prefer to stay home and assume the mother's role, and frequently carry on a homosexual affair, sometimes surreptitiously, but often with the knowledge of their wives. As far as the children are concerned, most love their father and don't criticize him for his sexual activities. They are not angry or resentful, but very unhappy if he leaves the marriage.

It is not unusual for a bisexual man to have suicidal tendencies when he is young, because he is torn both ways and adjustment is difficult. Most make a comfortable decision, however, some have trouble accommodating to the dual role and seek psychiatric guidance. They don't look upon either choice as wrong but want to know whether there is an advantage in focusing on only one.

The word bisexual is misused by both professionals and the public, claiming that if a man or woman has one homosexual experience, he or she is bisexual. This is erroneous, for many heterosexuals admit to a homosexual encounter in early youth out of curiosity.

WHAT ARE THE EMOTIONAL FEELINGS OF GAYS?

When gay and lesbian couples establish a relationship, how do they feel? What are their emotions? They fall in love, just as straights do and the emotions and feelings are exactly the same. This may be hard for a straight to swallow but it is the truth. Romantic love between a man and a woman is not limited to straights, strange as it may seem, gays experience the same sensations. A bisexual man or lesbian will corroborate this, for if he or she marries, both will tell you that it was because they are in love with one another.

Do gay couples ever get married? A few do and several small religious groups will marry them, but these marriages are not recognized legally. Gays, both men and women, feel that they should have the same civil rights as straights. The law does not agree.

There is another side to this coin. It is the nature of human beings to have children. This is one of the three basic drives, self-preservation, self-advancement and self-propagation. So gays want to have children as do straights and many marry and have a family.

DOES A GAY MAN EVER MARRY A LESBIAN?

Occasionally, yes—however, the nurturing instinct can be strong in both sexes and foster the desire for children, which is the motivating factor. In the marriage, the parenting is shared, but sexual activity is with those of their own sex.

It is interesting to know that there are a few instances of a "menage à trois," which is an unusual phenomenon whereby two gay men and a lesbian live together. One threesome pooled their resources, bought a house and moved in for the purpose of bringing children into the world. This illustrates the strong drive to have children although all three are homosexual.

Soon a little girl was born to the woman and was well-loved and nurtured. No one knew which of the two men was the father. They did not want to know. The four lived as a family, the mother continuing her relationships and the men theirs. Presumably, the child grew up normally in a loving family, although to date there has been no follow-up.

SOME GAY MEN MARRY

When a gay man marries, and he is not bisexual, why does he when he only loves men? And what sort of woman would marry him? From the man's standpoint, it is usually for money, social, advantage or to hide his homosexuality. She is willing to put up with considerable mistreatment and often rejection.

The woman who marries a homosexual must accept that he might be an inadequate husband in many respects, not only sexually. Some gays present the worst characteristics of males and females, combining aggressiveness and bitchiness, and can be very unpleasant when challenged. Some make adequate fathers, but most lack real feelings for their wives, who serve only to close gaps in their lives. The woman who loves a homosexual will continue to grieve about his infidelities and his lack of love for her. This he is incapable of doing, but she never accepts it.

This unusual woman's family background falls into a classic pattern. Her mother is extremely paranoid and not interested in children. She makes a poor mother and more often than not has only one. Her husband is a passive, well-meaning man, artistic and sensitive, who allows his wife to rule the household. His personality lets him bend to his wife's demands, ensuring peace. So this woman has inherited a unique combination of personality traits.

GAYS ARE NORMAL, HAPPY PEOPLE

Most gays are comfortable in their roles and are mature, happy and well adjusted to life after each individual has made his or her place in society, however, each must always be mindful of the forces that prevail in criticism of their sexual orientation. This remains a burden on every gay soul. Although they are subject to mood swings and anxiety as are many heterosexuals, most don't go to psychiatrists for advice, but those who do, go for reasons other than their sexual orientation.

As homosexuals grow older, they are pitied for their lack of family and apparent loneliness, but a recent study by the National Institute of Mental Health reveals that homosexuals of both sexes feel quite comfortable about aging. While most don't have close family ties, they all have good friends and involvement in an interesting field, and many live with their lovers more compatibly than in their younger years.

CHAPTER SIX
The Political Impact of Gays

A BIT OF HISTORY

Why is it that the subject of homosexuality is so popular in the media today? This emphasis on sexual orientation appears to have emanated from an event in New York City in the summer of 1969 known as Stonewall, and has burgeoned ever since. Prior to this the states had been repealing their laws on sodomy and discrimination against gays in housing, employment and insurance. Furthermore, a movement for civil rights for gays had been gaining momentum for years when Stonewall precipitated it into full bloom.

What happened? On June 28, 1969, the New York city police staged a raid on a gay bar called The Stonewall. They entered and began harassing the men there. Several hundred gays gathered outside and began fighting the police for trying to move them away and a full fledged riot developed. This group personified the millions of gays who had been pushed around and abused by the police for years.

In this manner the momentum reached a climax and what is now called the "gay liberation movement" began. Subsequently, out of the group emerged a small gathering of activists who by being visible and vocal gave the impression that all gays wanted to separate from straights and have their own society. This is not the case but was the impression that was portrayed. All the majority wanted, and still does, is to live equally in society without social stigma or legal discrimination.

Although it took almost twenty years, small groups across the country valiantly sallied forth in order to inculcate the general public that homosexuality is not a disease, is not a choice, but that those who are so "inflicted" were born that way. An example is a happening in 1988 in Hartford, Connecticut.

A gay man was beaten to death by two high school athletes and his body left on the front lawn of his house. They explained that they did this because they "hated fags." This infuriated a group of young gays in the area so they decided to draw up a plan to fight back. They chose a non-violent strategy to inform the public about homosexuality. Subsequently they formed the Stonewall Speakers Association dedicated to explaining homosexuality and what it is like to be gay, and to make the public aware of the discrimination and abuse they endure because of their sexual orientation.

The organization is made up of volunteer men and women and all necessary funds come from their pockets. They are not involved in fund raising. They visit high schools and businesses about the state with the objective of stopping violence and hatred against gays and to acquaint the public with the facts about homosexuality.

Is this a national organization? No, and it is not even statewide, however, there are similar groups in New Haven, and in Massachusetts, one is in Boston and Northampton. Undoubtedly, there must be many more about the country.

It is unfortunate that the subject of homosexuality entered the political arena and in such a destructive manner. During the last campaign for the presidency of this country, none other than the then vice-president attacked the gay community, vilifying all gays and lesbians as having chosen an "alternate life-style" which he claimed to be "evil" and that this life-style is unacceptable. In retrospect, could the anti-gay attitude of Bush himself have influenced the voting against him?

Could it have been Clinton's espousal of gay rights and gays in the military which was markedly apparent during his campaign for the presidency that tipped the scales to ensure his election? Moreover, it is well known that large amounts of money were contributed to his campaign by gay groups. We may never have the answers to these questions.

AT LAST THE SUBJECT IS AN OPEN BOOK

After the elections in the spring of 1993, up to a million people marched on Washington in support of equal rights of gays and lesbians. Those involved comported themselves in an orderly and dignified manner. Petitions to the administration and Congress were presented asking for recognition as a minority group with the same privileges as other people.

Furthermore, there was a good deal of campaigning for Clinton by gay enthusiasts as well as financial support and, for the first time, the gay and lesbian community was actively involved in a presidential race. They entered politics in a big way and the gay vote may have been decisive, especially in critical states.

Before the 1960s and 1970s, both male and female homosexuals had no forum from which to exert political pressure on the heterosexual world, which had oppressed them, ridiculed them, and denied them their constitutional rights of free speech, assembly and other civil liberties. The only place they could congregate was in the gay bars, where they were able to speak freely with one another about political issues. There were no rallies for the gay community and no political groups or lobbies.

DRAG OPENED THE DOORS

In the bars, drag had its place and gradually drag shows began to appear, capturing the group's attention and building a sense of identity and belonging. Here, gays could share their frustrations and air the constant rejections that they were subjected to daily. So, over the years, they developed into a strong entity, dedicated to ameliorating the negative attitudes they faced every day. They yearned to be accepted as individuals and respected for what they were and not reviled for their sexual orientation.

Thus, the concept of "drag" as a political tool began in the gay bars and finally emerged into the open and the streets, resulting in rallies, parades and so forth. These activities helped to eradicate the feeling of isolation and of being different, a concept that had been thrust upon them and with which they had always had to live. By the 1990s, gays had gained access to the more traditional segments of the power structure and established their own churches and clubs and organizations.

THE GRANTING OF CIVIL RIGHTS

The next forward step is the legal establishment of civil rights for gays. Conditions have improved somewhat, as a few states have passed anti-discrimination laws and the recognition of the rights of individuals, but nowhere do gay couples, male or female, enjoy the privileges that the rest of us take for granted. The religious and civil ceremonies of marriage cannot be performed on gay couples, and the courts don't recognize their relationship in legal matters. For example, gays have no protection in housing, jobs, health insurance or even the military, from which they are discharged if their sexual orientation is discovered, but President Clinton is changing that.

It is under such a burden that all gay persons live, and there is no major culture in the world that so severely penalizes homosexual relationships as in the United States. There are laws against sodomy, buggery, perverse or unnatural, acts, crimes against nature, public indecencies, indecent public behavior and so forth, and the penalties are more severe when an adult and a young person are involved. Only one state condones homosexual relations in private between two consulting adults.

It is interesting to note, however, that these laws do not seem to apply to lesbians because no females have been prosecuted under them.

RESEARCH AND POLITICS DO NOT MIX

It is strange that medical research can have political implications. Nevertheless, when a medical scientist discovered that a tiny portion of the part of the brain that regulates sexual activity is smaller in homosexual men than in heterosexuals, the press immediately grabbed on to this news and reporters speculated about its influence on gay rights. Another research finding points to one or more genes that may predispose men to homosexuality, but this has yet to be corroborated by replication. From these findings evolved the political impact of homosexuality on social and public policy, because of the now proven role of nature over nurture as the physical cause of homosexual orientation.

Most scientists are unhappy about the commingling of research and politics and would prefer that their work be kept separate. When research discovers a definitive biological cause of homosexuality it will go a long way towards advancing the gay rights movement.

THEN CAME AIDS

In 1981 the religious right was jubilant in announcing that God had brought upon mankind a scourge to destroy the evil of homosexuality and that the gay and lesbian community would be wiped out. Soon it became obvious that this was not to be as AIDS became widespread. AIDS is a scourge of global dimensions attacking every group, male, female, old, young, every ethnicity, nationality, color, race, creed and sexual orientation.

It is a fact that in the beginning AIDS was most prevalent in gay males, then in certain locations in the country most frequented by them, but the myth that gays were the only targets was quickly dispelled when it soon became obvious that everyone is vulnerable.

The tragedy of AIDS brought into the open for the first time the attention of society to a minority group that had been largely invisible and powerless. It united the gay community and caused its members to rally and evaluate their strengths and weaknesses as have other minorities in our society. These groups had nothing to lose and much to gain by speaking out, for they were highly visible and usually congregated in communities, but gays had to remain invisible in order not to risk losing family, job, social standing and friends.

However, once the disease was identified, the gay community worked diligently to decrease the incidence among its members by abolishing certain sex practices, and this effort has proven to be highly successful.

Billions of dollars are being devoted worldwide to find a cure and better treatment than we now have. So far these efforts are discouraging, but eventually a cure will be found. There are many studies being conducted with experimental drugs on AIDS patients, the results of which will not be known until they are concluded and show promise. Moreover, there are indications that there may be another strain of the virus that causes the disease because there are a few HIV positive cases who have survived without treatment for up to fourteen years without developing full blown AIDS.

In the meantime, abstinence from sex, monogamy or "safe sex," (the use of latex condoms) are the only recourses for the prevention of this dread disease and this last method is far from sure. In addition any exchange of tissue among individuals, such as blood transfusion of organ transplant, must be carefully monitored, and IV drug users must use clean needles.

CHAPTER SEVEN
Gays I Know

THE GAYS SPEAK OUT

Of the gays I interviewed some were friends, some were strangers. Every one of them was more than willing to see me and to cooperate in every respect. They all seemed anxious to share their feelings and experiences and to get them out into the open. When asked to testify, every one responded enthusiastically in the affirmative with no reservation and, although each was promised anonymity, not one asked for it.

THIS IS BOB'S STORY

"I remember being attracted to men even before adolescence, when I was four or five years old. I have always felt that homosexuality is not so much a sexual preference and a life-style that one chooses, but that it is hereditary, a part of your genetic makeup. I have always been curious as to why I am gay and what made me different from the rest of the guys, so a few years ago I went to a doctor to have a DNA test, purely out of curiosity. Preliminary testing revealed that I had more of the X than the Y chromosome. This was very interesting but it was enough for me and I did not pursue the testing further.

"Several times, I have been asked if I want to change to heterosexuality, but I have never, never wanted to even think of attempting to do this. Perhaps my case is unique because even before I came out, I knew I was attracted to men more than women. However, I always had female friends and never discriminated, as some gays do, for whatever reason, a bad childhood or realizing their mother is a woman. I find that some gay men resent women and I have never done that. In my case, most of my friends are gay men and gay or straight women. I don't choose my friends because of sexual preference or for any other reason.

"There is a gay bar in my town I like to visit occasionally on a weekend. The management wants to attract people on weekday nights so the bar will become more popular. Interestingly enough, their modus operandi is to advertise in a manner that attracts a gay clientele. They believe this will enhance their image and the place will become trendy. So they are advertising it as catering to an alternate life-style.

"Many straight people are homophobic. I think this belongs with the other kinds of prejudice, such as to blacks, Jews, etc. If one is prejudiced, that person is prejudiced usually to the whole list. People who are secure emotionally and open minded don't have this problem and don't allow it into their lives.

"My family did not know I was gay until I came back from college in 1971. None of my siblings are gay as far as I know. I have a brother and a sister, both of whom are married with children. I have another sister who was in a convent for six years and then left. She lives alone and works for a doctor. However, I have always had a feeling that she is gay but I have never asked her and she knows that I am.

"You asked if I am out of the closet. I suppose I am but I don't go around announcing it, but if someone asked me I would be honest about it. I am comfortable with myself and accept others for what they are and who they are. And no one has ever asked me if I am out of the closet, but if anyone did, especially in a professional environment, I would feel that it was none of their business. I think it is important to keep myself detached personally when in a professional environment. However, in a social setting, I really wouldn't care and this has never been an issue.

"I am totally homosexual, not bisexual. I don't really understand being bisexual because I think there is something lacking in the person who is. I never had a desire to marry, ever. I did think about it once, but I knew that it would be a failure. Twice I could have been engaged to a girl for there was a love there and a bond, but not based on sex. It was more emotional. I love kids but having them would never suit my life-style, which is to live alone and be independent, and I can enjoy my nieces and nephews. I have never for even a second felt that I am missing out because of not having children."

Bob is in his late thirties; he is outgoing and talented. He has held jobs as a hotel desk clerk, a bank teller and a ballroom dance instructor.

JUDY IS A LESBIAN

"As far back as I can remember I never went for boys, but always put myself into the 'going for boys' status because it was the thing the other girls did. I knew, however, around the age of fifteen or sixteen, that I was different. About that time I transferred schools, and have a particular memory that still stays with me. It was about the gym teacher, Cindy, who was very attractive and feminine. She wore makeup and lipstick and had long painted finger-nails, her hair was frosted and she wore little short skirts.

"I used to think about her at night, but in this fantasy it wasn't me. I was a man spending time with her but it wasn't sexual because I knew that was wrong, so the fantasy never reached that level, but my mind and I were completely inside a male body. Then, at some point I became aware that there was something wrong and it should be me in my own body spending time with her. Then I realized that I had a unique connection to certain women that I never really put in a sexual perspective. I just wanted to be around them, however, it was not that I never wanted to be around guys, but just never had that feeling about them which was unique with women.

"I came out of the closet under rather unusual circumstances, a little different than the average. I was a sophomore in college and it was a free time for both of us, and I didn't know the words, the phrases, the lingo or the bars and the clubs out there. I thought we were the only two people on the planet that were having this relationship, and very, very naive we were, physically and emotionally. It was like way out at left field, and nothing that I had thought about or read about or talked to anyone else about. In fact, I was quite surprised by it, but nothing ever matched the reaction, emotionally or physically, that I had with a woman. So that is how it sort of evolved, very quietly, very subtly.

"I wasn't raised where I was in a position to find out. I could have gone to the library or picked up a magazine or newspaper. I was in a large college town where there were a number of universities and colleges so I think if I chose to pursue it I could have, but I didn't because, number one, I didn't want anyone to know that I was acknowledging certain things to myself. I went back to my tenth college reunion a number of years ago and the people that I thought about over the years had come to relationships later. A whole bunch of us realized that we were hiding from each other, but we were aware of each other. As you put the pieces together years later, you realize Oh yes, those two! They were even then. And a few of us started talking and being up front and honest about what was going on in college. I went to a catholic college and there were nuns there and I definitely knew that there were several pairs of nuns that were inseparable, and I found out later that they had their relationships.

"Back then we didn't have the words, such as gay or straight or heterosexual or homosexual. I don't like being called a lesbian, I don't like the word, the sound of it, the S and the B sound. It is a hard and abrupt word. I like the word gay and when you say "gay" you can mean a man or a woman, but they always refer to the gay and lesbian this or that. Most men refer to themselves as gay and women as lesbian but most of the women I know refer to themselves as gay.

"I think some of us thought we were clever in that we dated men and got married in order to erase the fear of being discovered, the fear of the future and the rest of life. I was in the military, the Army, when I met my husband. There was so much fear in the military about being gay. I loved what I was doing, I loved my job. And I really coped out when he asked me to marry him. We hadn't slept together or anything, we had been dating about a month and I told him about some very special female relationships in my past and it didn't phase him or bother him. However, about a year into the marriage it bothered the hell out of me. I couldn't continue to live like that. It is not fair to someone you really love and do care about to find every creative reason possible to avoid sex. It is just not fair. He had a right to a woman who loved him as a wife. We talked about it. I told him that I felt trapped, that I couldn't stay this way. He said we can stay married and you can do your thing on the side, but I said no I can't do that either. When I recall it he was a very nice guy, and wanted marriage and kids and the whole bit, but I couldn't go that far. So we got divorced. I don't know where he is and never see him. It is better that way. But I am glad I got married. I would have wondered how I would have been in a marriage if I hadn't. Now I know that I can't emotionally do that. My whole reaction to sex with a man was so radically different than sex with a woman. It is unbelievable.

"My mother just did not want to acknowledge that I am gay. Mainly, because everyone seems to think that the life-style is so terrible, so lonely and hard. There are aspects to it which are but there are aspects that we treasure. I finally got her to realize how I react this way physically. Also it had to do with the way I was raised, the fear of pregnancy was very serious. I guess I felt that there was no sharing. When I was with a man I was like a vessel, just something there for him. With a woman it is so mutual, so unbelievably together. I never felt physically used by a woman, it was so give and take.

"When I was fourteen, I was raped, but I don't believe that was a deterrent to me toward being with a man. However, I think that it stuck with me emotionally so that I could never be comfortable or trust being with a man, not ever with my husband who was wonderful and I didn't distrust him, but I just didn't feel that we were there together at the same time.

"I have these lines drawn in my mind and I cannot fuse them in any way. If a man says something nice to me, I ask myself what does he want? If a woman says something nice to me I take it more graciously, more honestly and openly. I don't know where this comes from it's just there. Sometimes I rue the fact that I am gay, for society is cruel. I resent the fact that there are career paths that gay men can openly be gay in and all is OK, and knowing that there is a job for him that he can go into and it will be perfectly fine. If anything, it may enhance it.

"What do I do? Drive a truck? The stereotypes are still high for women, but we don't have certain outlets as the men do. True, we can hide it more easily, but every day at work I have to put up with the comments and the flirtations and you can't say, back off, I am not interested. For if you do, it doesn't stop the comments and makes you more of a challenge. Then you get into the trap of being asked to get together with the rest and go out on the town and you know what that leads to.

"What did I do in the military? I was a television producer and had an important position in broadcasting for the largest network in the world. I loved the work and apparently was good at it. However, I was turned in as being gay by a lover and when I had to admit it, I was told that they knew and condoned it. A lot of this sort of thing went on in the military when a man or a woman was doing a good job. The authorities were often aware but could not ask you and unless you were turned in by someone as I was they passed it by. This went on all the time but if someone is turned in or admits it, that person has to be discharged. So I had to resign and was honorably discharged.

"After I left the Army, I joined with the rest in the march on Washington in 1979. There was a huge crowd, much more than the press admitted. In this regard, I firmly believe that there are many more gays than the ten percent of men and two percent of women that the authorities claim."

TOM WAS AWARE AT SEVEN

This is what he told me: "As a child around seven years old, I knew that I was different. I didn't know what it was but I knew there was something. I did not know my sexuality at that age but felt instinctively that I did not react to life as the other boys did or feel as they did about things.

"I matured very early and when I started to go through puberty, I had more of an interest in men and was attracted much more to men than to women. That was when I was about twelve or thirteen. At that time I was surrounded by men, male teachers, male priests, and males all around me, but I still didn't know what it was all about, such as my lack of interest in girls, when so many of my friends began to date girls and talk about them.

"I just didn't understand why I was different, and actually, it was very difficult to accept considering my heritage and my religion, which was boy meets girl, falls in love, marries and has a family. At that time, I thought that I was probably the only person in the world like this!

"I was about eighteen or nineteen when I had my first experience and became aware of my sexual identity. This was extremely difficult to accept. I was very innocent but it was interesting to realize that someone cared for me other than the close members of the family who really do care. Then my lover left me and we did not see one another for many years but became friends again but never had sexual contact. Then he married, for whatever reason I will never know.

"After that experience, I put myself into a shell as I felt it was bad for me and I should not indulge myself that way. Then I became introspective. I punished myself for submitting to this man and becoming involved. At the time I felt that it was going to be a relationship that would be long lasting because he had told me that he had been looking for such a relationship for many years. I understand now that he is still looking!

"As far as my parents are concerned and my brothers and sisters, I think it was understood and it never bothered me or them. They were so beautiful and they accepted anyone. I used to bring friends home and if I was attracted to someone I always brought him home. That was very important to me because my home was my life. It was everything and there was never a word uttered. My father accepted everybody, my mother was never phased in any way. I don't think my brothers and sisters ever said anything. They perhaps realized but it was never a problem.

"I am a very private person and I was always struggling for my true identity. I am not a bit aggressive, and maybe I should be but that is hard for me. I don't have friends I go out with. I bring them home, for that is the place for me. One of my brothers is bisexual and he has his own apartment in the house, and we go pretty much our own ways, except at work and when we go home to our parents. But now they are gone.

"When I go to New York for my work, I meet people but always stay apart and don't encourage making friends, although I know they are gay also. I had an affair with one man who was married, and it lasted four years and ended in disaster. Some years later we met again but did not resume the relationship, however, remain good friends. That is the way with all my affairs, which are not very many, and they all walked away and broke my heart. I don't know why.

"I have always wanted to find someone with whom I could form a permanent relationship and spend the rest of our lives together. I yearn for that."

MEL WHITE'S SECRET

Mel White's story was depicted recently on the television show "60 Minutes." He was familiar to several individuals of the religious right for whom he ghost-wrote their autobiographies. They did not know that he was gay.

Mel is a bisexual, but did not know it. He had what he called an affliction which he firmly believed he could rid himself of by leading a normal life dedicated to Christian beliefs and values. His parents were fundamentalists and he was a priest of the fundamentalist church, which teaches that homosexuality is evil and all gays will lose their souls, be abandoned by God and go to hell.

When Mel went to college, he tried to live up to the Christian life he was brought up in, only to find that he would rather hold hands with a football player rather than a cheer leader. In his zeal to prove to God that he was heterosexual, he struggled to achieve and was an exemplary student. He won many prizes and was elected to every student body office.

He thought marriage would cure his condition and soon he fell in love with a girl he had dated as a teenager. They married and raised two children, all the time Mel believing his marriage would cure his condition. He did not realize that he was gay but simply thought he had a problem.

Then something happened in Mel White's life. He was installed as dean of the Cathedral of Hope in Dallas, the largest church in the nation which caters to the gay community and welcomes straights as well. Now, Mel could stand up and say: "Thank you, God, at last I can tell everyone who I really am. I am gay, and proud of it, and God loves me." At last, he was free to be himself.

Early in the marriage, he had told Lyla about his problem and they decided to work together to cure it. So, through the years Mel endured exorcisms, electric shock therapy and aversion therapy. At first he felt a therapy was helping, but after a few months the old feeling returned to haunt him. Then he became suicidal. He told Lyla and she was shaken. She persuaded him to seek professional help and he finally overcame the desire to end his life.

Finally, after twenty-two years of marriage, they consented to divorce, but remained close, loving one another and gathering as a family on holidays and special days. Mel loves Lyla, his children, his home and all that goes with a family, but could no longer pretend to be heterosexual.

I KNEW WHEN I WAS FIVE

Roger told me this story: "I knew I was gay before I entered the first grade. I didn't know the word 'homosexual' but I somehow knew that I was different. Then on the playground, I would hear the word 'queer,' 'pansy' and 'gay' and when any of these words were used I knew somehow that they related to me. However, I really didn't have the right word for my sexual orientation until I was in the fourth grade.

"I had an instinctive knowledge of what sex was about but it was all very fuzzy and confused in my mind. I was not the only one who was all mixed up about it, the other boys were also, but they knew somehow that the mystery would come to light when they married. That was the mentality back in the fifties when I was growing up, but I knew it would not be true in my case. Life promised only loneliness, fear and hiding, and when I die, my religion tells me that I will spend an eternity in hell.

"One day when I was about ten, I could stand no longer not knowing why I was so different from the others, so I decided to ask the coach. I stayed after class and when the others had left asked him what the words 'queer' and 'pansy' meant. He seemed surprised and uncomfortable and said they were words for a homosexual. When I asked him what a homosexual is, he said abruptly, 'look it up in the dictionary.' So I went to the library and Webster's dictionary, but could not make myself take it off the shelf. I felt that everyone was watching me. Finally, my heart pounding, I had the courage to open the book and found that the word homosexual means 'someone who is attracted to members of the same sex.' This certainly was me, but the description went on to other words, such as 'pervert,' 'deviant,' etc., which I had to look up also. These words had terrible meanings and certainly did not fit me. I had always been obedient and did what I was told and believed everything a grown-up said was true. I was ten years old and beginning to understand a little.

"Having acquired this knowledge about my condition, it didn't help me very much, for I was so very alone and there was no one to share it with, nor did I know that there were others just like me. All I ever heard from my peers and from grown-ups was derision and criticism.

"As I entered high school, I would hear my peers tell jokes about going to parks or bars where homosexuals hang out and lie in wait and attack a person whom they thought might be gay. This pastime was fun to them and was known as 'rolling homos.' No one seemed to care about the person they attacked, not even the teachers and coaches. Even the police laughed and joined in the 'fun.'

"I felt so terribly alone! I couldn't even share my fears with my parents, who were kind and loving and whom I loved in return. And I was so afraid. During this endless period of growing up, never once did I see or hear a person speaking in favor of a homosexual. Without exception, it was always an unequivocal condemnation and hatred. So how could I tell my parents? What would they do to me? They could have no choice but to disown and abandon me. In my young mind, I would be left with no family, no home, no friends, and no means of support.

"So I resigned myself to what I assumed would be a life of horror and loneliness and fear, and to pray for God's help to hide my secret until the day I die."

ALEX IS BISEXUAL

"I was not aware of my sexuality until I was in puberty. I never had any desire to have sex with anyone. However, I discovered when I was in my early teens, there was something that attracted me to other men, but I always had a strong inclination toward women as well. I think, basically that my spirit is more on the feminine side than masculine. But I don't want to be a woman, I never desired to be a woman or have a sex change or dress up like a woman. I just have stronger feelings towards men, emotional as well as sexual.

"I was twenty-eight years old when I first experienced sex. It was with a woman and then a man at about the same age. I guess I was a late bloomer. As I got older and was more active with men my desire for women diminished. Now, it is only men. I never married but when I was about twenty-five, I had a very strong desire to marry this young lady. I was very shy and we went on a couple of dates. Then she met this other young man and is happily married twenty-eight years later. We remain friends but she never knew how I felt.

"Because of my heritage of being Italian and Catholic, all this talk about sex is taboo. In the beginning, I had a very difficult time, because the so-called normal thing to do was to marry, and for many years I toyed with the idea, but then I started to be somewhat active with men. There was a lot of peer pressure and family pressure and you almost wanted to say, I'll get married to please everybody, but I couldn't do that. I wouldn't do that for myself nor for the other party involved. It was just too deceitful.

"How about my parents? We never discussed my sexual orientation. My mother may have known because she was very intuitive, but we never really discussed anything about sex. My father has been deceased for twenty-two years and we had a good rapport, but we never discussed sex. My mother was more open and broad minded and I think if I had discussed it with her she would have understood. And I know subliminally, that she had some inclinations and knowledge about me. But she was very happy, I think, that I never married, although she mentioned that she would like me to, but I think she was happy that I was still home with her.

"In retrospect, if I had married, she would have been happy as well and I think we still would have had a close rapport. Only in the past three or four years have I been open about it. However, there are lots of people now who are more open about it so it is easier to discuss and people are accepting bisexuality and homosexuality more now than ever. Clinton did a lot to bring this out with his 'gays in the military,' and the press picked it up and is having a field day.

"Of my siblings, one sister knows and she is open and accepting. I think the other members of the family know as well, but we just don't talk about it. If a sibling confronted me with it I would reply but I don't think it is necessary for me to announce it. I don't have a lover, but if I did it would be more noticeable.

"As I said, I had my first sexual encounter when I was twenty-eight and up to that point, when I was in my late teens and early twenties, I had a very strong inclination to enter the seminary for the priesthood. I was serious about this but my mother was against it, so I really didn't pursue it as much as I should have. Perhaps it was not a genuine calling. I don't know. But the reason I didn't engage in sex all those years was because of my religious belief. I have always had the philosophy and the belief that whatever sexual orientation one has, you don't do it until there is a commitment.

"When I began to have sex, I learned very early, fortunately or unfortunately, that I would like a one on one relationship, but that is not the case. That bothers me to this day. I would like a one on one commitment, a happy one and for good, a fulfilling relationship. It has always been my belief that when you fall in love and make a commitment, it should be monogamous. That is my personal belief but I don't think it is reality. I have had my share of flings and one night stands as one calls them, but then it is only a physical thing. Two people are attracted, they do their thing and you might see them twice again and then they go their separate ways and that is that."

MELINDA'S STORY

"It was when I was eleven or twelve that I seemed to realize that I was different from the other girls. I will have to say that at this age of thirty-eight, I am totally gay. It is very interesting because it seems that the stronger my self-image becomes, the more I tend to have a normal life-style but I don't know if I could truly go through with it. When I was in my twenties I dated quite a lot and I had intercourse with a few men, but I think the more I engaged in intercourse, I disliked it more and more.

"I think I have finally come to understand that I became gay because of my childhood background. I do believe that I strongly disagree when people say genetics, I think it has to do with self-image. I feel that because I had a low self-image as a child and a very poor father figure or male figure. There was no male figure in my life and when I did come across a male, it was through hatred and resentment. When I moved out of home when I was seventeen years old, I felt that dating was just dating another male, not a friend, and he was categorized as just a male. I think this is the reason why I really am what I am.

"I probably could change if I had the same amount of time that made me this way. Sometimes I want to change. I feel that all of my life I have never been accepted. I think I had it tough as a child and tough in school also, and I don't think I was ever given a chance to be accepted. And, in answer to your question, I would like to change to be accepted as being 'normal.' Because I always feel abnormal even though in my heart it is right. My master is my heart, I know nothing else. So I go with that. It seems as though I am a pretty stubborn individual and I do what I believe in and I know I would be ostracized at work.

"I come from a big family of seven and my family does not know that I am gay. I adore my mother. I kiss the ground she walks on, truly. She is a wonderful woman but I know that if I ever told her, she would still love me but she would put guilt on herself. I would not want that to happen to her because she would blame herself. She would think that it is something she contributed to and if she had done things differently things would have been different. But she never asks me about my life, which is a nice respect.

"My father is a very, very odd man. He and my mother are from the old school and don't believe in divorce. I think for me, psychologically, my being gay stems from my Dad. He is a very mentally and physically abusive man and I think from not having a good strong self-image, I think possibly that is a little why I am. He abused me but not sexually. He hit me. I have come to a good acceptance of things from the past and letting them go and staying where they should be. And it doesn't infringe on my daily life. Sometimes, I think I shouldn't say it but I think I have gone past the stages of anger and possibly hatred toward my Dad. I have come to acceptance and am trying to understand him and why he was what he was at that time.

"My Dad is not any nicer to me now. It is like he has come to premature senility in a sense. It is like he has never been there, you know. I think he approached a nervous breakdown when I was in my teens, but he never really came out of it. He just stays to himself and we have accepted this. He is a very fortunate man because he has seven children. We grew up in a ghetto area of Syracuse, and have some of the principles we grew up with, such as good morals and good values. He has a very good family, none of them are alcoholics or drug abusers. I have to say I am the only black sheep, but you know, sometimes I think of myself as special also. I mean even from my name Gaye, I get razed about it by people in general. It is the topic of jokes because it is very uncommon.

"None of my friends know I am gay. I have a few such as Diane, who is the best friend I have ever had in my life. She has so many good qualities that you don't find in a lot of people. She is good hearted and a good worker."

MANY FAMOUS PEOPLE ARE GAY

History tells us that a goodly number of the most famous people were bisexual or homosexual. This information applies mostly to men, although no doubt there were famous women as well who were homosexual. The reason for this is that women throughout the ages have been relegated to an inferior position and due to the fact that male homosexuals greatly outnumber lesbians.

As already mentioned, in the days of ancient Greece, it was the accepted norm for men to have sexual relations with young men and boys. This was the way of life for men as a means of appeasing their sexual appetites. This was true of Alexander the Great and Plutarch. Socrates, the philosopher, was a close friend of Alcibiades and it was widely known that he was intimate with him. Plato, also a philosopher, was a disciple of Socrates. All these men were married and had children. Julius Caesar was married three times, but was known to welcome sexual relations with anyone who was available and willing, man or woman, young or old.

Moving along in time, there are the famous Italian artists, Leonardo Da Vinci and Michelangelo, both of whom were both sculptor and painter. Leonardo's most famous painting is the Mona

Lisa and he was also an accomplished engineer. Michelangelo is widely known as a sculptor for his "Pieta" and as a painter for the ceiling of the Sistine Chapel. Both men most probably were bisexual.

Nearer to our time was Oscar Wilde, perhaps the most openly famous homosexual. Somerset Maugham and Andre Gide were bisexual. However, until the end of the twentieth century, society refused to accept homosexuality. Just as the word "cancer" never appeared in the public press back in the 1930s, so is the word "homosexual" omitted today when referring to an individual. Now, the tables are beginning to turn.

Let us move up to times we are more familiar with and the famous people we know of. Here are known homosexuals, some of whom may be bisexual—actor Rock Hudson; a celebrated champion figure skater; Nureyev, the dancer; Liberace, the pianist; a well-known activist in government and business, J. Edgar Hoover; and author Truman Capote.

There are many more, too numerous to list, that are emerging into recognition and acceptance. Although it is not possible to confirm, most of those we have mentioned are probably bisexual and it is becoming more and more apparent that a large segment of the general population relates to both sexes at some time in their lives.

As I finish this manuscript, the twenty-first anniversary of Stonewall is being celebrated in New York City where it originally took place on June 27, 1969. Thousands of gays from all over the world are marching up Fifth Avenue displaying a mile long rainbow banner dedicated to the liberation of the gay community. The mayor of the city and other celebrities are marching with them. An atmosphere of joy and happiness prevails and there is no protest and no disruption. It is like the parade of an ethnic group which takes place from time to time in this great city throughout the year. This parade is simply a continuation of the efforts of gays to gain understanding and acceptance in this country as they have in other countries.

www.ingramcontent.com/pod-product-compliance
Lightning Source LLC
Chambersburg PA
CBHW022016080426
42733CB00007B/619